GET MORE LIFE
OUT OF YOUR
BUSINESS

Greg Weatherdon

Copyright © 2013 Greg J. Weatherdon
All rights reserved.
ISBN: 0992077400
ISBN 13: 9780992077402

Table of Contents

Foreword

Business ownership is a dream for many and a reality for few. I was fortunate to have realized my dream and benefited greatly from the experience and in the process reaped its rewards. Unfortunately, that is not the outcome for most entrepreneurs who tempt fate as the majority fail to achieve success, let alone a livelihood.

Regardless of the current statistics, there are still millions of business owners who have proudly created something from nothing more than an idea and hard work. The fact that they are able to pay their bills and earn a living is a testament to their abilities. What they don't realize is that they're in the minority. They are in charge. They are in control of their destinies. Good or bad, failure is based on the decisions they make.

Being self-employed entails many sacrifices without any guarantee of success. Those that do survive and flourish seemed to have the resilience hardwired into their DNA. They say you learn more from failures than your successes and that is certainly true of being an entrepreneur.

Unfortunately, many who for all outward appearances can be considered successful, have yet to achieve one of their most important goals for going into business: Freedom! Granted they have all the physical trappings that come with financial success, but many are handcuffed to their businesses that they don't have the time to enjoy everything they have achieved.

My objective in writing this book is to get you to think a little differently about your business and to take away at least one idea that will get you closer to your goals.

Introduction

**"Dream big, but don't forget to execute.
The dream keeps you motivated,
hard work makes it happen!"**

-Greg Weatherdon

The Dream

A business begins with little more than an idea, a vision and plenty of enthusiasm. Growing that idea from day one into a thriving business with a list of successes and happy customers is a common dream. It's what many people aspire to. But it takes a special person to actually throw caution to the wind, ignore the naysayers and disbelievers, and turn that dream into a reality.

Small business owners are some of the hardest working people around. Why? Because they have to be. The first few years of a business' life are difficult, challenging and come with the requisite sleepless nights, headaches and long hours. There are many great books about starting your own business and guiding it through its fledgling years as a start-up. This book isn't one of those.

Getting more life out of your business means taking a hard look at how your company works and how you manage it. By making changes so your business runs without you, you will have achieved what so few business owners have managed. The positive impact this will have on you, your family and your life cannot be understated.

This book aims to help small business owners answer the question "what's next?" and help them -- you! -- get all the benefits of being the owner of a thriving company. Every entrepreneur becomes self-employed to realize a dream. That dream usually includes the following reasons:

1. to gain independence
2. to make more money
3. to have more vacation time
4. to achieve a better work/life balance
5. a desire to build something, etc.

Unfortunately, we as small business owners get in our own way of fulfilling those dreams by not being able to step back and help our companies get to the point that they run just fine without us. Pride and ego can keep us from becoming happy as owners because we let other people's definitions of success cloud our thinking.

It's easy to confuse who we are with what we do. We have duties and responsibilities within a business, but it's not who we are, it's just something we do. And people lose sight of that. We often tie too much of our identity to the business.

On top of that we frequently forget that just because we are the owner, we're not always supposed to be the hardest working person in the organization. We need to step back and manage rather than do.

Will your business ever get to the point that you can kick your feet up on the desk and do nothing at all? No, probably not, because having nothing to do is just the ideal. But the closer you get to it, the better off you'll be, because you will have achieved what so few people have in running their businesses -- freedom of choice, freedom to decide what you want to do every day of the week because your company will be working for you instead of you working for it.

Now that you've made it through the challenging start-up phase, it's time to shift your focus to becoming a business manager and begin focusing on the long range goals and less on the day-to-day minutia. It's time to **Get More Life Out Of Your Business!**

objectives

think / Act on **1** idea

1- Passion vs excitement

↑   ↑
message   getting a Job
from the job

2- Do what you say you will do

3- Build it to sell it (65% don't sell)

Challenges - Leadership - conductor Image
                        sales   online vis.
                profits   Life

don't Life out of desperation -

Teach them -   80 Results Profits
                                         Revenue Problems
Pareto   ───
  80%/20 Principle   20 efforts
                                       customers
                                       products
                                       employees

Sales facts
- 80% - no fallowup
- 44% given up after 1 time
- 80% you can after 5 call
- Touch Points - stay in touch with past clients

Sales tactics
- identify decision maker + influencer

$\frac{80}{20}$ customer talk 80%
   - you 20%

3 - ask for the order / job
4 - Yes - stop talking when you get to Yes for a sale

Sales oportunity
- Networking - Chambers
- coffee a week - make a list + meet with one person a week
- Online presence - 85% use Online
                     65% read reviews

Social media
   - good to bad - a tool
Life - what are you doing it for

- time to think
- time for yourself
- keep your promise

Define your own sucess

1

Get Your Business Organized

"We are able to do anything we want if we put our minds to it. But first we must decide whether it should be done at all."

-Greg Weatherdon

It's Time To Evolve!

The small business owner's hat rack needs plenty of hooks. Not only do you wear the hat of president, but you fill many other roles in your company -- the top-level executive positions of vice president of sales, marketing, operations, finance and human resources, right down to sales administration and shipping/receiving roles. If you had one, your company organization chart would look like this:

Today

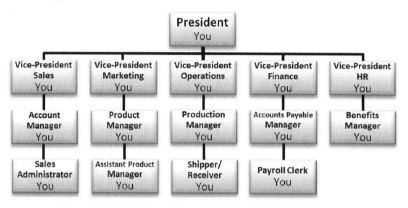

Although wearing so many different and varied hats was likely a necessity when you began your business, chances are you're still wearing all those hats even now that your company has grown out of the start-up phase. Why?

Once a business has grown and staff has been added, many small business owners fail to relinquish or delegate responsibilities to employees. The net result is you end up with a dysfunctional organization whereby you're in a constant state of being overwhelmed, and your staff is not only unproductive, but also highly inefficient because they are waiting on you to provide them direction.

Trust is a big factor in business, and failing to trust employees with your "baby" can lead to stress, overwork and too many unnecessary long hours at the office.

Your Ideal Company

Ideally, you want to get your company organized in such a way that you hand off many of the vital roles you previously played to trusted employees so you can focus on very specific roles and larger strategic issues. Not only does it put responsibility in the hands of others, freeing up your own time and letting you enjoy the benefits of being the boss, but it also makes it easier to sell your business at a later date because the company's success doesn't fall entirely on your shoulders.

When I advise business owners to delegate more responsibility, inevitably people tell me there's no way they could delegate important roles to their current staff members. Perhaps they're right that their current crop of employees aren't capable of handling roles like production manager or accounts payable manager, but they could likely handle some of the individual duties within the larger roles. Give them some of those responsibilities and you may be surprised at the result. Delegating even a few day-to-day duties could free up a significant amount of your time while sending a clear message that your employees are a trusted part of the team.

All organizations have these key roles, and chances are you are filling most of them, which not only requires more effort than you need to put into your business at this stage in its lifecycle, but also places undue burden on you and the people around you.

Believe it or not, you're not supposed to be the hardest-working person in your company. The business owner's role is to manage and oversee the operations of the company, not to do everything. At the beginning, sure, you may have had to wear every hat in the business at one time or another, but once you've built a sustainable business, it's time to step back and let the business -- and its people -- run themselves.

Upwards of 85% of businesses fail by the time they reach their fifth anniversary. If you've made it to the five-year mark, congratulations are in order because you've beat the odds and you have emerged out of the start-up phase and into the next phase of your business. The hard work of your first three to five years in business has reaped the benefits of a living, breathing and viable business, but odds are you're still running and managing your business as if you're still in start-up mode.

With trusted people filling the roles that make your business run, you can afford more time to yourself and for your family. Remember all those vacations you said you'd take when you began your business? You'll be able to take those, and you won't have to worry about your business collapsing because you're gone. That's why your goal is to have your organization chart look like this:

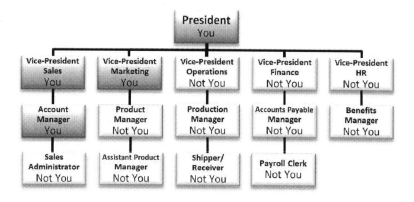

Tomorrow

| | | President | | |
| | | You | | |

Vice-President Sales	Vice-President Marketing	Vice-President Operations	Vice-President Finance	Vice-President HR
You	You	Not You	Not You	Not You
Account Manager	Product Manager	Production Manager	Accounts Payable Manager	Benefits Manager
You	Not You	Not You	Not You	Not You
Sales Administrator	Assistant Product Manager	Shipper/ Receiver	Payroll Clerk	
Not You	Not You	Not You	Not You	

2
Get Your Business Working For You

"Are you working for your company or is your company working for you?"

-Greg Weatherdon

Maximize Your Potential

Knowledge is a powerful thing in every aspect of life. In running your business, knowledge gives you more focus and a greater understanding of what you're doing right and what could use some improvement. By taking what you've learned through analyzing your business and your customers, you can maximize the potential of your business and focus on the activities and customers that provide the highest returns. The net result is that you create a stronger business and take a major step towards setting your business up to be more predictable. And isn't that the goal of every business owner?

Follow The Money

Once you understand your business and your customers, you should be far more confident in making decisions related to revenue and profit. If you've done the work and gone through the process, you know where your strongest profit centers are, and you can now focus on those areas of your business that are generating the best profits, cutting out the areas showing weak or no returns.

Business owners often waste a lot of time and energy on activities that they know are only marginally profitable because they don't want to lose an order or a customer. The problem is that we continually justify accepting these projects because we are under the mistaken impression that some profit is better than no profit. The fallacy of this way of thinking is that we rarely take into account the wear and tear on equipment or cash we need to tie up to complete the project. If we did take these items into account, we would quickly realize that instead of having a project that is marginally profitable, we end up losing money. To make things worse, while you've been busy on this marginal project, you've probably missed out on other projects more suited to your area of expertise. My advice is: When faced with these kinds of decisions, let your competitor have that project. That way they'll be way too busy chasing that little trickle of money, leaving you to concentrate on more profitable activities.

Believe it or not, it's perfectly okay to focus your business on the most profitable areas and remove services that aren't worth the time and effort. It's a no-brainer to cut out low-margin services from your business. The only exception to that rule is if the low-margin service is an add-on to a high-margin service, in which case the weaker service is necessary to keep the stronger service running. In this case, the low-margin product or service should rarely, if ever, be offered as a stand-alone service.

However, there exists another option for the low-margin activity -- and that is to outsource it. At The Marketing Resource Group (MRG), one of the services we offered was direct mail marketing. We did about $200,000 a year in this area, but the margins were razor thin. To compound the problem, we were only called on infrequently to execute a direct mail marketing campaign. Due to the nature of the business, we had to commit a large portion of our office space to offering the service. So we were effectively heating and lighting an empty space that we rarely used along with equipment that was dormant between uses.

I learned quite by accident about a company that only did direct mail. They focused strictly on doing the final step of direct marketing campaigns (collating, stuffing and sealing envelopes, verifying addresses, applying postage, sorting and finally delivering everything to the post office). In speaking with them, I quickly learned that since this was their specialty, they were able to do the work cheaper than we were. It only made sense to outsource the work to this company and they became a strong supplier and partner in our overall business. The added bonus was that we increased our profit margin while doing very little of the work, and reducing expenses.

The lesson here is: Had we continued performing the direct mail services in-house, we would have been forced to purchase additional equipment and commit even more real estate to the service -- real estate that was sitting idle for three out of every four weeks.

MRG's core competency was not in direct mail, and when I discovered a company we could outsource that service to, it was an easy decision to make. From the clients' standpoint, nothing changed. We still handled the project and billing, but handed off the campaign execution to a third party.

As owners, we sometimes don't consider alternatives because we're worried what the client might think. What if they find out you that you don't execute all the services in-house? First off, they'll probably never find out;

and secondly, if they do, most won't care, because at the end of the day they want results. When you can provide them with what they want hassle-free and at competitive rates, that's what customers **really** care about. Let me reiterate: You should **ALWAYS** be looking for alternatives to your non-core or mission-critical activities.

Here's another example, courtesy of a landscaper I met. He was talking about wanting to buy a Bobcat for his business. A Bobcat is a small, versatile and highly maneuverable front-end loader, and a decent used one will set you back about $15,000. I asked him why he wanted to buy one, and he responded that he thought it would help his business.

As we talked, he confirmed to me that he really didn't have anywhere near enough work to justify the purchase, but still wanted one. I then asked him what he currently did when a job requires the need for a Bobcat. He responded by telling me that he had a deal with a company whereby they provided the machine and an operator for $85 per hour. To my way of thinking, this seemed like a great arrangement. So I then proceeded to ask him why on earth would he want to spend that kind of money, to say nothing of all the additional costs of maintenance, fuel, insurance, etc., when you can rent it as you need to, with an operator to boot? He really didn't have much of an answer other than to say he wouldn't have to schedule the rental and would have it whenever he needed it.

I suspected it was more of a pride issue than a practical one. But this is exactly the kind of thinking that gets many business owners in trouble and adds undue stress to their lives. Yes, there may be a time when it becomes necessary to own that piece of equipment, but doing so prematurely, because it's a point of pride, is never smart business.

Take a look at your own company's low-margin businesses and investigate your options. You really only have three choices:

1. Do nothing and continue running them in-house.
2. Outsource them to an organization or individual that has the expertise and can do it cheaper.
3. Stop offering the service.

No matter how much you'd like to, some services simply can't be outsourced. In that case, you really need to spend time to figure a way to make them more efficient. Maybe you can find a way to automate them or simplify the process required to deliver the service or perform the task.

This approach is not limited to only big processes but should be performed across all areas of the organization on a regular basis. All gains in efficiency go directly to your bottom line, regardless how small.

Look for ways to improve the efficiency of the services you offer, but also understand that some services will never reach critical mass or generate enough revenue and may need to be terminated.

Although I've only discussed outsourcing or streamlining products or services you offer, this thinking should also be applied throughout all areas of the organization. A good example of a process that every business with employees has that can be outsourced for little cost is payroll processing. When I ran MRG, my vacations were limited to no more than thirteen days at a time because either I or my wife had to be back to run payroll and sign the checks.

Occasionally, we could manage slightly longer vacations, but that required producing payroll advances for our employees. It created a lot of extra work, for a few extra vacation days, and quite frankly, rarely worth the effort. I don't know what took so long -- and I'm talking years -- to discover that outsourcing payroll processing was hardly any more expensive than doing it ourselves. In fact, it may have been cheaper because they also took care of making all the government payroll submissions and produced other payroll-related paperwork.

By outsourcing payroll, it provided us the freedom to take longer vacations or to be away from the office during the payroll cycle because we had out-sourced the function. And that's the purpose of doing all this work -- to make your business work for your lifestyle rather than the other way around.

Document Processes and Procedures

It happens all the time: An employee moves on to another job elsewhere, and suddenly there's a gap in knowledge related to processes and proce-dures. Something as simple as logging into or updating the company web-site suddenly becomes a not-so-trivial task.

This problem relates back to a business owner's challenges in stepping back and not being the be-all and end-all of the business, but in this case, it's an employee that has left the company -- and, through no fault of their own, has left the business in the lurch.

The solution to this is simple, even if the execution may take time. Every recurring task within an organization should be documented in detail so that if the person responsible for that task is suddenly no longer there, there are processes and procedures in writing others can follow to accomplish that same task. Although documenting every procedure may seem like a daunt-ing task -- because it is -- start with those tasks that are mission-critical to your business, the ones that would really ruin your day, week, month or year should any of those individuals responsible for those jobs leave your employ.

Everything from how to conduct a telemarketing call to what goes into a holiday voicemail message should be documented to keep operations at peak efficiency and show a potential buyer of your business that your company is running smoothly.

Not only will this go a long way towards selling your company, but it will also make life at the office easier and more enjoyable. In many cases, you may find better ways to do things while you're documenting your procedures, which in turn will save time and money.

The Two-Question Test

It never fails. When speaking to a group of small business owners and entrepreneurs about how they can get more life out of their business, there's often someone who tells me they can't step back from the day-to-day management of their business. Their role is too critical or they can't trust their employees. There's always a reason.

My response is to ask them two questions to give them the proverbial "slap upside the head":

1. Can you phone your business and tell them you're not coming in for the next month and for them to take care of everything?

2. What happens if tomorrow you have a heart attack that lays you out for three months?

It's all hands on deck during start-up mode, and perish the thought the owner is ever sick, but after start-up mode is over, it's important to keep in mind what happens if disaster strikes. Making sure the business can operate without you is win-win for everybody. It means happier employees, a smoother running company, a better work-life balance for the owner, and an attractive, purchasable property.

Adapt Your Services To Other Industries

Sometimes it takes a happy accident or an objective eye to see that a product or service tailored to one industry can have a much wider range of uses.

Take, for instance, the famous story of the invention of the Post-It Note. The glue on the back of the Post-It Note was originally intended to be a super-glue, but when the glue proved to have little adhesive properties, it was abandoned. The eureka moment came when the chemist used the adhesive on pieces of paper to mark pages in a hymnal at church without leaving any residue. 3M, the owner of the Post-It Note, didn't immediately see the genius in what would become the product for which the company is arguably best known, but in time, the sticky note became a staple of offices everywhere.

How can you take your own products or services and adapt them to industries you are currently not serving? If you run a restaurant, can you offer catering services, or how about a daily delivery service to that office tower down the street? If you own a bakery, can you supply local restaurants with fresh bread and desserts? Of course, these are simple examples, but by stepping outside your current mindset you may be able to uncover unique opportunities.

Not that creative? Then gather up a bunch of customers or trusted business associates and offer them a free lunch to help you brainstorm. The fact that these individuals are not in your business could prove to be a boon to your idea-generating activity because they don't have any mental restrictions that you may have developed over the years. This kind of activity can be very motivating and enlightening. This is exactly why you need to free yourself from your business so that you can spend more of your time undertaking these activities.

There's No Such Thing As A New Idea

With the constant demands of running a business, it's always a challenge to stop for a moment to consider if something can be done faster, better or cheaper. Most of the time we're just happy to get the work done, get paid and focus on the next project or order. Because of this, we run the risk of adapting the "it's always been done this way" attitude when someone makes a suggestion for improvement.

Your working environment may also hinder possible ideas coming forth for efficient gains. How so? Well, for starters, have you encouraged the people you work with to come forth with their ideas? If so, do you seriously give them consideration or do you just go through the motions of listening to them? I certainly don't think for a second that every idea is good or can be implemented, but having a workplace environment that encourages and expects suggestions is a great starting point to get your employees to embrace the concept. Just remember there are no stupid ideas. They can be the genesis of an even bigger opportunity.

There are a number of reasons why you should take the time to look for efficient gains. To begin with, the fact that you've been in business for a couple of years suggests that you have existing customers buying your products or services on a regular basis at your current pricing. What if you could increase your margin, the money you make, by an extra 2, 3 or 8 percentage points? Wouldn't that be reason enough? Alternatively, what if increasing your efficiency now allowed you to compete more effectively within your industry because you have more pricing power? Would this not be a good thing?

Unfortunately, what usually takes place is that we tend to look at the big picture and focus on finding that one big thing or piece of equipment that will make us more competitive. What if instead we focused on streamlining 5 to 10 things we currently do? Unlike buying that new piece of equipment that has an initial or potentially long-term cost, improving how we currently do things has virtually no cost associated with it. It's like finding free money.

Unlike large corporations that may have designated staff responsible for finding the latest and greatest technology, the typical business owner must rely on their powers of observation to find low-cost improvements. A great starting point is to simply look at how you're currently doing things and see if you can remove unnecessary steps from the process.

Maybe it's no more than reconfiguring work space to make task flow smoother. Asking questions, like why is the printer located on the other side of the room? Wouldn't locating it closer to those that use it the most make more sense? Sounds lame? It's this kind of thinking that starts the process and when nothing is too little to improve efficiency, bigger and better ideas start to come forth. Every little gain in efficiency is like putting money in the bank.

But don't stop there. Adapting or borrowing ideas from industries outside your own can help you save time, money and ultimately increase your productivity. The following is one example of how I managed to change how we did things simply by borrowing from another industry.

The Peanut Butter Directive

In running The Marketing Resource Group, I learned the lesson about adapting processes from other industries from watching a television show on how peanut butter was made.

One of the services we provided our customers at MRG was a fulfillment service. In a nutshell, a fulfillment service is as the name suggests. Our clients' customer would place an order for various marketing collateral to be displayed in store -- or for patient counseling, in the case of pharmacies. So every time we received a request or an order, we needed to count out a specific number of brochures, letterhead or whatever was requested, then package everything up and send it out by courier. It sounds simple enough, because it was.

As simple as it was, there was no standard order quantity, so counting out the requested amount of each item became a time consuming and tedious process for our staff.

So one evening while watching this television show on peanut butter production, I noticed that the empty jars were moving along at high speed to the filling station. As the jars were positioned under the filler tube and began to receive the product, the jar began to lower until it was full whereby the product stopped being dispensed until another empty jar made its way under the dispensing tube.

For some unknown reason, it became a eureka moment. Not knowing how the process worked, I surmised that the jar stopped being filled when it hit a certain weight because that's how the product is sold. I honestly don't know if the filling process stopped because of the weight or from some other trigger on the assembly line, but I didn't care, as I'd found a solution to improve our fulfillment business.

The very first thing I did when I went into the office the next day was I went looking for our old postage scale. Once I found it, I proceeded down to our fulfillment area and began weighing various counts of the marketing materials we were sending out for a specific client. I then recorded the weight of the various counts I was making. From that point onwards our production staff didn't need to count out thousands of mailers over the course of their day. Instead, they weighed the individual item until the scale showed the desired weight of the requested quantity and then packed them up for the client.

A couple of things happened as a result of that little change. First, we improved the work our people were doing. Let's face it, counting marketing material all day can be boring, so any improvement was welcome. Secondly, we managed to increase our margin on the business. To begin with, it is traditionally a very low-margin business and the only reason we were doing it was because it was an add-on to other more profitable activities. Lastly, this increased efficiency allowed us to improve our pricing to our customers, but also improve our margins.

By keeping my mind open, I found a way to improve our processes that benefited both the business and the client.

How A Big Company Saves

Money By Doing Little Things

Many years ago I became fascinated by how small changes could improve efficiencies after reading an article in the Harvard Business Review. The article profiled UPS, the package delivery company on how they looked at everything they did with an eye to improving efficiency.

Although most of us aren't in the delivery business or have their resources, the lessons to be learned are numerous. Their attention to the small things helps UPS to become an amazingly efficient organization in delivering millions of packages a day.

Early on, UPS determined that making left hand turns took longer to make than right turns, so they began routing their drivers' deliveries to minimize left hand turns. The route planning ensures less wasted time sitting at intersections, keeping drivers more productive. The up-front planning to make this happen must have been quite complex, but the end result was a more efficient system.

UPS also came up with a few other simple tricks to speed up deliveries. If you look at the driver's side seat in UPS delivery trucks, you'll notice the front-left corner, for left hand drive vehicles, is tapered in a way that makes it easier and faster for the driver to slide in and out of the saddle.

Another novel and no cost idea they implemented is when a driver stops to make a delivery they put their key on their baby finger so they don't have to fish around in their pockets each time they return to the truck. When you consider how many deliveries they make in a day, this simple -- and I repeat, no cost idea -- must save them an incredible amount of time. You don't need to be UPS to apply this kind of thinking to your business.

UPS is so obsessed with productivity that they are looking at converting their vehicles to do away with keys and provide the driver with a fob they attach to their belt. Once installed, the driver will simply use a push button to start the vehicle and unlock the cargo area. It is estimated that they will save 1.75 seconds per delivery.

Each individual productivity saver may only account for a few seconds of time, but over the course of a day, a week or even a year, it adds up to significant time savings. For UPS, they estimate the key fob will save them $70 million a year. The list of things they do in the name of increased efficiency is simply amazing.

Never Stop Looking To Improve

As you look to improve your processes early on in your business' life, it's easy to find ways to make things better. Increasing your company's efficiency by 15% should be relatively easy as you pick off the low-hanging fruit. Once the easy process improvements have been made, though, there are still likely many ways for you to improve your processes, your products and your services. Don't just stop when it becomes a little challenging. Engaging your employees in the process will certainly yield a far greater number of opportunities than you even realize.

Another example I implemented in my company was to automate our quote process. Prior to automation, it would take me approximately one hour to prepare a typical price quote for my clients as they all had to be customized. After realizing that it could be streamlined, I spent a few days working on a basic spreadsheet model that incorporated all our costs and margins. It also accounted for fixed overhead as well as forcing me to attribute a cost for items that I usually took for granted and assumed were covered by margin.

Once the variables, such as quantities required, were put into the spreadsheet, specific fields from the spreadsheet were then automatically linked to a word processing document that we sent to the client. Once implemented, this new quote process allowed us to prepare a quote in 15 minutes or less; and many times, they were completed and emailed while still talking to the customer on the phone.

By developing this simple process, it significantly reduced the amount of time required to prepare the quote. It now accounted for all our costs, which improved our profitability, but it also allowed other individuals in the company to prepare pricing for our clients and free up more of my time.

Another model I encourage you to look into is the Japanese concept of kaizen, or never-ending improvement. The concept originated following World War II when American occupying forces brought in Dr. William Edwards Deming to conduct management training using statistical methods. The simplest explanation is that Deming helped Japanese industry to learn to measure performance, determine how improvements could be made and then execute on those improvements. When done correctly, kaizen is a team-based process done on a daily basis.

When Deming went to Japan, the world considered Japanese products to be of inferior and often very poor quality. Using kaizen, businesses increased their productivity, efficiency and quality to become one of the powerhouses of the industrial world -- particularly in electronics and automotive.

Similar to kaizen is the Motorola-developed Six Sigma management strategy, which follows a similar train of thought in incremental process improvements. Whether you follow kaizen or Six Sigma, simply keep your mind open to new ideas for inspiration for how you can improve your business.

An efficient organization will keep you on your path to being able to enjoy the lifestyle you've always wanted as a small business owner.

Get Your Finances In Order

Long before ever owning a business, I often wondered why what seemed to be successful and profitable businesses would go bust. However, once I took the plunge into the entrepreneurial world, I soon found out why. In a word, cash flow.

For the majority of us, cash flow was a major issue when we first started out as we scrambled to get revenues up to a level that exceeded expenses. That, of course, went hand-in-hand with the challenge to collect on the receivables in time to pay the rent, payroll and credit cards.

Cash flow problems should end once we graduate from start-up, but for far too many of us it remains a daily challenge. Having the ongoing stress of chasing receivables, robbing Peter to pay Paul and prioritizing which payment to make is a major distraction from running and growing our businesses. At the end of the day, constantly struggling with cash flow seriously restricts your ability to get more life out of your business.

As I said above, I quickly learned the value of cash flow with my first company, The Sales Support Company. During the eight years I spent running this company I struggled constantly with cash flow. It's part of the reason I lost interest in the business and ended up selling it for just enough to pay off my business loan.

Because of the long lead time on client payments, we relied on a bank over-draft to keep us going each month. With 150 employees to pay and clients to satisfy, in what was a low margin business, this overdraft often topped $100,000 each month. This overdraft was a necessary evil, as, unfortu-nately, the employees needed to be paid every two weeks and yet some of our receivables were in the 30-60-day range. In hindsight, another reason that compounded the need for the overdraft was the fact that this company was severely under-capitalized from the start and the cash flow couldn't support the growth.

It was a delicate balancing act that eventually came crashing down. In the meantime, a business I had invested in using the same bank went bank-rupt, and the bank called in my thriving business' overdraft. They gave us 20 days to come up with $120,000. If not for a fortuitous break from a cli-ent who asked us to pre-bill a significant portion of an upcoming project, the lights at The Sales Support Company may have gone dark right then and there.

If all this wasn't stressful enough, I was still facing a dilemma. On the one hand, the bank, through its actions, was going to effectively close down my business. On the other hand, I was sitting in my office holding a six-figure check that was going to solve our immediate problems. So what was the dilemma? Because the clients' project wasn't due to begin for another three months, I had to make sure we were still going to be operational and solvent when it came time to do the work. Just because I could satisfy the bank's demand didn't mean we still didn't have a cash flow problem.

So unless I could guarantee we could complete the assignment, I wasn't going to cash the check.

To solve the problem, I called a meeting of all the office personnel, account managers, supervisors, etc. and showed them the check. They were aware of our situation, so they thought all was good. I then proceeded to explain that unless we could guarantee to complete the client assignment, I wasn't cashing the check. Because I didn't own a crystal ball, I advised them that this guarantee meant that they may risk their own paychecks to get this done. I promised that all our field staff would be paid, but that's where it ended. To their credit, they all agreed that the check should be cashed and they promised to see the project through.

We finished the project, everyone got paid and the company was back on its feet, but by this point, I was done. Running this company was a heck of a lot of work, and after eight years, I still wasn't taking a regular paycheck. That is when I decided it was time to sell The Sales Support Company. As I look back, I can probably give you dozens of reasons why I sold this company, but none would hold a candle to having insufficient cash flow. Cash is king, and don't let anyone tell you differently!

When I started my next venture, The Marketing Resource Group, I vowed never to struggle to make payroll again, including my own, and to never repeat the mistakes of the past by having an overdraft to cover receivables. This was accomplished in a number of ways, which I'll discuss below, but to summarize, I significantly sped up receivables and matched our growth to our cash flow.

Although bank credit for small to medium businesses has been significantly restricted over the past few years, having a bank loan or credit facility may be unavoidable. If that's the case, my advice is to keep it to the absolute minimum required -- and preferably only as a safety net. My point is regardless of the lender, you will have a payment schedule to keep, interest to pay and the need to abide by imposed covenants.

Change The Rules

As I mentioned above, when I started The Marketing Resource Group, I vowed never to endure the cash flow-related issues of my prior company. So in order to survive and prosper, I needed to seriously rethink how I had managed our billing and receivables process.

Installment Billing

The first thing I did was to initiate installment billing. At The Sales Support Company, I naively billed the clients 100% upon completion of the project. This simply compounded our cash flow problems. So from the very beginning of MRG, all clients received an invoice for 50% of the estimate the minute they approved the project. In many cases, the project wasn't scheduled to begin for upwards of 4-6 weeks from the time they approved it. So typically we got paid an amount equal to our costs prior to even beginning the projects. For new clients, the 50% had to be paid upfront before we did anything. We didn't even schedule the project until the check was cashed. What was surprising was how little resistance we faced in demanding 50% upfront considering that many of our clients were classified as Fortune 500 companies who can easily dictate the rules as far as supplier payments. Sometimes all you've got to do is ask.

Still not convinced? During this period I also started a media company, producing 10-second closed captioning and promotional consideration television spots. Due to the very large six-figure dollar value of the agreements and the commitments I had to make to the television networks, I demanded that the clients pay 100% upfront regardless of the campaign duration, many which ran the entire year. What made this so unique was that this industry is controlled by billion-dollar global media powerhouses that had established industry standards of billing their clients on a monthly basis. The point is, changing the rules is still possible but you won't know until you try.

Service Quotes Were Estimates

Once again the lessons learned from my first company served to force me to think how I was going to avoid past mistakes and significantly improve not only cash flow but profitability. With The Sales Support Company, I only billed what I had quoted. Why I did this is not totally clear, but I think it was because I didn't want to appear to be nickel-and-diming the client. In many cases, I had naively allowed clients to make minor additions to the programs without any changes to the original quote. Of course, any major changes required adjusting the quote. It was the minor changes that really hurt, kind of like "a death by a thousand cuts" that just ate away at our margin.

So to correct this, we clearly stated on all our quotes: "This is an estimate only and final billing would be based on actual cost incurred." At first blush, you may think that none of your clients would accept this as we could become very careless and inefficient to the point we would just run up costs. First off, taking advantage of our clients would not bode well for long-term relationships, but more importantly we had a couple of solutions.

First, we provided our clients with fairly detailed service estimates outlining all setup costs, supervisory hours, staff hours, overhead contribution, etc. By implementing this kind of transparency in our quotes, it increased our credibility and strengthened our relationships with our clients. As an added bonus, many of our clients requested any competing supplier to resubmit their quote and provide the same detailed information -- something they were unaccustomed and reluctant to do.

Secondly, we got pretty good at estimating. Approximately 98% of the time, our final billing was at or below the estimate, and in those rare occasions that we exceeded the original estimate, it was accepted without issue. Our estimating performance gave us credibility and gave the client the confidence to trust us.

For the 17 years that I owned The Marketing Resource Group, I never once had a cash flow problem or worried about making payroll. As matter of fact, the banks were calling me to see if I needed any financing. Look at the cash flow rules in your own industry. Don't be afraid to try and change them.

Put Your Business On a Cash Diet

When a business is flush with cash, one of the temptations business owners have is to spend it -- a new company car, new office furniture, modern art prints for the office or what-have-you. Also, a business with a plump bank account risks losing the fear factor that drives the company forward as complacency sets in.

One strategy I used at MRG was to reduce our cash balance by 50% once a year. It may sound a little strange, but this money was moved to secure and relatively liquid investments. Once removed from the company's day-to-day cash account, it became an out-of-site, out-of-mind situation and served to keep us hungry. I kept enough money in the company so we didn't have to sweat the details or desperately chase new business, but there wasn't enough money to drop it on a new toy or to get lazy. Basically, I put MRG on a cash diet.

Another reason to put your company on some form of cash diet is that as you get comfortable, you start to add small expenses to the business that individually don't amount to much, but over time start to really add up. But because you added them a little at a time you lose sight of how much weight you've added to your profit and loss statement.

It usually starts simply enough like giving employees cell phones or car allowances, but before you know it, you're spending thousands of dollars a year on unnecessary things for your business. All because you had too big of a cushion in your bank account and assumed rightly or wrongly that because of their small amounts, you'd always be able to handle them.

Carry A Balance

Some people will tell you that sitting on a surplus of cash in your business is a waste of money and that you should constantly be reinvesting the excess back into your business. I disagree. Just as you would in your personal finances, your business is only helped by having a bank balance that can get you through at least three bad months.

Another reason to keep a cushion is that it will keep you honest. One of the realities of running your own business is that you're going to be faced with periods of drought where business is going to be slow, whether as a result of seasonality of your product or because of economic reasons. So, by honest, I mean you need to have sufficient funds available so that you are able to stick to your plan and not be forced into scrambling to find some business. If you recall from a previous chapter, you should target your ideal customer and focus on your high-margin activities. By not having a decent cash balance, you risk veering off target and plan and start looking at projects that are not ideal only to be able to generate revenue. Plus having some form of cushion allows you to sleep at nights.

Bill Regularly

I run into this all the time and I have to admit that I've been guilty of it myself. Small business owners sometimes get too wrapped up in the operations and production of their businesses that they neglect invoicing. One of the quickest ways to avoid cash flow problems and generate incoming revenue is to be disciplined in your invoicing.

Another step that is often neglected and results in late payments is to follow up on your invoices with a phone call to make sure your client received it. Invoices frequently go missing and with so much electronic or email invoicing they frequently get overlooked. A quick phone call to the recipient will confirm they received it. By doing so, you'll also avoid a shock when you phone looking for payment 30 days later only to find out they never received the invoice.

I also recommend that you talk to your clients' accounting departments to find out what are their policies and procedures. This serves two purposes. First, you now have a contact in the accounting department at the client's company, and secondly, they may give you some insight as to how best to send invoices to ensure prompt payment.

I adopted this policy a long time ago, and one client, who was a global manufacturer and good for the money, was a chronically late payer. Upon talking to the accounting department, they advised me to not start a project until I received a purchase order number and to also send the invoice directly to their department, as it then became their responsibility to chase down the required payment signatures. As for the purchase order number, what I didn't know was that my contacts at this company typically didn't process the purchase order until they had received the invoice adding to the delay in payment. Once I adopted these procedures, we were never faced with a late payment again.

Issuing invoices to clients in a timely manner should be a priority. You'd be surprised at how many businesses fail to learn this basic rule of business.

It's Okay To Say "No"

If you constantly have overdue receivables from an existing client, it can become quite a chore simply trying to get paid. Don't be afraid to stop doing work for them until they're current in their bills. It sounds drastic, but if you don't put your foot down, they'll just keep taking advantage of your generosity. It could also be a sign of trouble brewing at your client's organization. The risk of alienating a customer far outweighs the risk of doing all the work, incurring all the expenses and be left holding an empty bag.

Nobody wants to lose a customer, but always fighting to get your invoices paid is not a lot of fun and highly stressful. Trust your instincts. Sometimes it's best to let a troublesome client go.

Think of the bright side of letting a troublesome client go. They might just end up at one of your competitors and now make their life miserable.

Keep Your Finances In Good Order

Cash is the lifeblood of all businesses. Your year-end statements may show you're profitable, but without cash flow, you can't survive. So if you're struggling to keep cash in your business, change the rules and see what happens!

Expanding Your Business

If you think the grass is always greener somewhere else, chances are someone is looking at your lawn.

Expanding far afield, opening new markets, world domination -- they're all elements of expansion on the minds of entrepreneurs. It must be one of those inbred ideas that entrepreneurs have to be in a hurry to expand outside their local markets.

Not that this is necessarily a bad thing, but timing is everything. Doing so too early is a potential recipe for disaster. Too many owners get a bit of success and think they're invincible. What many ignore is that they may already be overextending their company resources and their staff. Add to that expansion plans and you could be looking at a disaster in the making, and everything you've worked for may suffer irreparable damage.

Stretching Your Resources

Not unlike a military operation, moving into a distant geographic location will stretch your organization's supply lines. If the location or territory is not adjacent to your existing geographic trading area, you end up putting tremendous pressure on your company, especially if it isn't properly structured to handle the absence of key staff during the expansion period.

Additionally, the operation side of your business could also come under pressure. Production lead times may now need to be increased to allow travel time, and your delivery vehicles may need to be redeployed to handle the new geographic area, typically resulting in higher costs and less effective usage.

Out Of Sight, Out Of Mind

Just like when you started your company, you were closely involved with its early stage development. Unfortunately, opening a new distant location requires you to take a major leap of faith with your newly-hired staff. With all the duties, responsibilities and stress of expanding, there is a very high risk of failing to communicate all your processes or to train the new staff completely.

Granted, you can always transfer a long-term key employee to take on the responsibilities of managing the new location, but -- if you're like most of us -- you don't have a spare manager sitting around. Not being there in the early stages means you can't immediately step in and correct any operational deficiencies before they turn into a major reputation or financial crisis like you did during your start-up years.

Vulnerability

While you're off conquering new lands, you risk exposing your base business to competition. Although you may think there are no threats to your business, you'll be far more distracted and enamored with your new project that you may not be aware of the poaching going on until it turns into a significant rout. By that time, the momentum may be difficult to slow down or, worse, you'll have to make a choice in where to spend your time -- new or old? You may be good, but chances are even you can't be in two places at the same time.

So When Is The Right Time?

The easy answer is: Never!

Chances are you'll never have all the pieces of the puzzle together. However, there are a couple of questions you can ask yourself to see if you are ready to expand outside your local market and tackle the unknowns of another pasture.

Do You Own Your Backyard?

One thing that requires very serious consideration before any thought is given to expansion is whether or not you are firmly entrenched in your current trading area, however big that is. By this, I mean, have you exhausted all potential prospects that are close at hand? This not only relates to geography, but also your identified target market or trade class.

Have Your Sales Stagnated?

In keeping with the above, have you reached a point where there really aren't any additional prospects? If you've done everything you can to increase revenue with little results, then maybe it's time to look further afield.

Can You Handle It?

Seriously, forget "pie in the sky" wishful thinking. If your business is running so smoothly and you're confident that your existing human and physical resources are capable of handling just about anything without your input, then maybe it's time.

The problem is knowing the difference between wishful thinking and strategic thinking. A hard look at the reality of your situation will hopefully tell one from the other.

The Decision is Yours

If you're honest -- and I mean really honest -- with yourself, and you answered most of those questions with "yes," then maybe your business has come to the point where it's time to expand. If, on the other hand, you can't honestly answer "yes" to most of the questions, then it's time to regroup. Take a close look at those areas where you may be the weakest, get them fixed and then reconsider expansion.

Just remember, if you're looking at potentially greener pastures, there is a better than even chance someone is looking at your lawn and thinking about moving in as a competitor.

Expansion can be a great way to grow your business, but it needs to be done in a calculated manner so that you don't risk destroying everything you've achieved.

3

Sales

No Sales, No Business

Much has been written about all the skills an entrepreneur needs to be successful. Being creative, action-oriented, risk-taker, visionary, opportunistic and resourceful, just to name a few. But in my opinion, the number one skill every owner requires, if you are going to have any chance of success, is the ability to sell.

It's surprising how many business owners try to avoid selling whenever possible. When challenged, they readily admit that they find it a very uncomfortable and a highly stressful activity. However, what they fail to realize is that by not selling, they risk compounding their stress levels when they have insufficient business to pay their suppliers, rent or employees. In others word, "No Sales, No Business!"

Selling has many definitions, but at the end of the day, selling is nothing more than the ability to convince someone that your idea, thought or product is better than the alternative. Selling is not high pressure, aggressive or confrontational. Nor is it a full contact sport where winner takes all, but more about finding common ground that allows the buyer and seller to agree that they have found the best solution.

Strangely enough, though, some of the best salespeople I've encountered will tell you they aren't salespeople at all. Yet their unassuming manner coupled with their deep passion and belief in what they're doing make them powerfully persuasive individuals.

So if you genuinely believe in your product or service, you're passionate about the benefits it can deliver and you are truly concerned about delivering quality results, chances are you can sell.

Yes, there are natural born salespeople, just as there are natural born inventors and athletes, but for the vast majority of us, we need to learn the skills we lack. The great thing about selling is that it can be a learned. Although you may never become a professional salesperson, your goal is to simply be able to sell well enough to create revenue for your enterprise until such time as you can afford to hire someone who can do the job better than you. Once this goal has been achieved, you can then spend more of your time doing the things you actually enjoy.

It's Only The Beginning

Passion and enthusiasm will only take you so far, but if you truly want grow your business, you'll need to grow your revenue, and the only way to do that is by selling more. The only way you're going to sell more is by getting better at it.

The days of high pressure sales have long been over. However if you look hard enough, there are still a few dinosaurs roaming around. For the most part, though, consumers in the Western world do not take kindly to this type of salesmanship.

So how do you get better a selling? Well, like anything else you want to improve, you'll need to invest some time in education. Unfortunately, there really aren't a lot of formal university or college courses that deal with selling, so it's pretty much up to you to create your own learning regimen. The good news here is that there is a wealth of information available online, in book stores and in your local library. This is how I learned when I initially started out. I devoured everything I could on the subject. At first it required a lot of reading, but as I discovered audio recordings, I could now absorb even more information any time I was in the car.

Alternately, there are many seminars and coaches that can help you. The biggest challenge here will be to find an individual whose selling style fits with your personality. I say this because as individuals we like to be treated a certain way, and to me, the old adage of treating people the way you want to be treated holds true. So it's imperative that you and your coach are in sync.

Strive For Success

It's an unfortunate fact of the sales cycle that 87% of customer inquiries are never followed up on by sales staff. Think about it for a second. How many times have you been told by someone that they'll get back to you and never do? How many times have you forgotten to get back to someone? Even if only one in 20 of those inquiries could have been turned into a sale, you've left money on the table. That's missing the low-hanging fruit.

Selling isn't easy and will take both learning and practice to master, but to make it work, business owners have to get out of their comfort zones and devote time, energy and resources to the sales process.

Sales success can also be measured, so you can learn from your mistakes and improve your own techniques. Have you ever tracked how many leads are required to get an appointment and how many appointments it takes to get a sale? Or how many customers that come into your place of business and leave without ever buying? How many buy? Do you track things like your closing ratio or the average value of every sale? That's the beauty of sales activity; it can be measured, and anything that can be measured can be improved.

Improve The Odds - Standardize Your Presentation

One of the jobs I took in order to improve my selling skills was to sell life insurance. It was one of the best decisions I've ever made. The sales training you receive as a rookie is second to none.

That training never did leave me, and one skill that I still use today is to have a standard presentation. This proved especially useful with new clients. Whenever possible, I used a PowerPoint presentation when introducing my company because it served many functions.

First off, over the years I had refined the presentation to focus on the services that were of most interest to my existing clients. Although we offered a number of ancillary services, focusing on our core offerings kept the presentation moving forward while quickly summarizing our secondary offerings.

The second benefit of having a standard presentation was that it insured all key topics were covered even if the presentation got derailed somehow. This happened frequently when I had to present to two or more individuals. Having a formal presentation allowed me to quickly regain control of the conversation.

Lastly, having a standard presentation allows you to refine your pitch to the point that you can present it blindfolded. This in itself has numerous benefits and none more so than your confidence in delivering the information. With this comfort comes the ability of watching the reaction of your audience to the points you're making without worrying about what you're going to say next. Making mental notes of these points will allow you to refer to them either during your presentation or afterwards during the conversation.

Be Pragmatic

Whenever you're in sales mode, make sure to speak to your customers about solving their pain points, not about the bells and whistles of your widget. Too often inexperienced salespeople get all hung up on how great their product or service is and forget to uncover the client's needs. Uncovering the needs of your client allows you to demonstrate how your offering can solve the problem. It's a common mistake and a waste of everyone's time to talk about product features that may not be important to the client.

Another common mistake made by the uninitiated salesperson is that just because you've been given an hour in front of the prospect, it doesn't mean you present for that long. Whenever possible, I try never to present for more than 20 minutes. The rest of the time should be spent on discussing specific client issues and opportunities.

At the end of the day, you must remain flexible. There have been many times where I've never finished my presentation yet have left with an order and a new client. It happens when during the presentation, the client gets an "aha" moment and runs with it. When this happens, my advice to you is to go with their train of thought and to heck with the presentation. With enough experience, you'll know when this happens. If it turns out to be a false alarm, you can always pick up where you left off.

Sales Equals Relationships

Why, when it costs between 5 and 10 times more to get a new client than it does to keep an existing client, do we often ignore our existing clients? I suspect it's because of the excitement we get when we land that new client, whereas dealing with an existing customer is pretty routine in comparison.

The sales process doesn't end when the contract is signed or the product is delivered; it's quite the contrary. In many cases, it's just the beginning of a long-term relationship. How you manage that relationship will dictate the impact that customer has on your future revenues. It is said that if you increase sales by just 5% from your existing customers, you can increase your profitability from 25%-85%. Why? When you think about the effort that goes into getting new customers, something we rarely quantify, keeping them as customers is so much easier. If everything went well on their first interaction with you, there really is no reason they won't do business with you again and again.

Building these kinds of relationships takes a commitment of time. To begin with, you need to be visible to your clients on a regular basis. There are many ways to accomplish this without leaving your office. It can be as simple as a phone call or an email. Ideally, though, in-person contact is usually the most effective, especially in business-to-business environments. Meeting with the customer at their place of business allows you to be visible to others at the company and serves to reinforce you as a supplier.

Don't fall into the trap of only chasing new customers at the expense of losing an existing one. Yes, new business is the lifeblood of every company, but don't confuse new business with new customers. Because the more customers are buying from you, the less you're having to sell, and getting deeply entrenched with your clients is always beneficial.

Leverage Your Customers

Business owners often miss opportunities because they don't properly communicate with and leverage their customers. Think about it: How often do you ask your customers for referrals? Many business owners would answer "never" or "rarely." It's something we're all guilty of not doing at some point in our careers, but failing to ask for referrals from happy customers is a missed opportunity.

Even though it is a simple process, most people are uncomfortable asking people for referrals from their friends, family or business associates. You have created credibility with the customer, and not to leverage that is a mistake because of the simple fact that people like to help others when they can. Additionally, a referral to a potential customer carries far more weight than a cold call and can dramatically reduce the sales cycle. Of course, there's also a greater potential of a referral turning into new business because people tend to refer you to people who may have similar issues or needs as they have.

There are also great ways to reward your customers for referring others to your business. A bakery, as an example, could place cards on the counter that offer a 10% savings incentive to existing customers who pass on an incentive card to a friend, who can also get a 10% discount off their first order. It's a simple way of maintaining a good relationship with existing customers while also bringing in new business.

Creating and sending out a newsletter, whether by mail or email, also presents an opportunity to stay in front of your customers. It's an easy way of keeping your customers informed about what's going on in your business, such as special offers or new services. I have a simple philosophy when it comes to newsletters: It cannot be purely company-driven propaganda but must also contain information that is useful to your client. Maybe it's a sales tip or a review on new software that is related to your industry or just a how-to tip. Just use your imagination, because if you want people to continue to read your correspondence, it better have something in it for them.

A newsletter's cost to the business is negligible but provides a simple way to remind your customers about your business and, if done right, you are perceived as an ally and not just a supplier.

Rejuvenate Your Prospecting

When was the last time you took a hard look at your prospect list and cleaned it up? As business owners, we have to be eternal optimists; otherwise, we would never make it through some weeks, let alone some days. As part of our day, we are constantly looking for new prospects, making sales pitches, following up and essentially going through the whole sales cycle as we try to generate revenue for our businesses. Of course, this is on top of all the other hats we are wearing.

As we go through this process, we accumulate a list of the most promising prospective clients based on the buying signals we received during our meetings with the hope that they will turn into paying clients. Needless to say, this list of prospects continues to grow the longer we're in business, and with it comes a false sense of comfort. I say "a false sense of comfort" because we lull ourselves into believing that all these prospects will convert to customers if we stay at it long enough and continue trying to contact them. And why not? The following statistics are often referenced and state that 80% sales are made on the 5th-12th contact.

2% of sales are made on the 1st contact
3% of sales are made on the 2nd contact
5% of sales are made on the 3rd contact
10% of sales are made on the 4th contact
80% of sales are made on the 5th-12th contact

Unfortunately, many interpret "contact" to mean the same as "attempted to contact," but there's a big difference! In this context, "contact" means to have a two-way conversation or correspondence with the prospect and not just leaving numerous unreturned voicemail messages or unanswered emails. So if you're not getting any response or acknowledgement from your efforts, your perseverance is most likely a waste of your time.

So to avoid thinking that you have a boatload of legitimate prospects that may, should or are going to buy, I suggest you cull the list on a monthly basis to only those that you are really having some form of dialogue. Those that don't make the cut go on a separate list to be contacted some day when you really don't have anything else to do.

The downside of this activity is that you're going to realize that you have far less in the sales hopper than you thought. The goods news is that it just may scare you enough to rejuvenate your prospecting activities to fill up your pipeline.

Talk To The Right Person

Making a sales presentation to someone who can't make the final purchase decision can end up being a waste of time. In business-to-business sales, save yourself time by making sure you're dealing with the decision-maker in every sales situation.

You may get an inquiry about your services from someone other than the decision-maker who has been charged with doing preliminary vetting of a supplier. If you qualify, you may be asked to come in for a meeting. During the meeting, it's quite acceptable to ask who will make the final decision. It may be the person you're meeting with or it could be someone else. This is information you should know. If it's someone else, find out if it will be possible to meet with them before the final decision is made. This needs to be handled tactfully as to not insult the person you're meeting with.

In a business-to-consumer setting, it's often clear who the customer is, but sometimes in a retail environment, two or more people come in together. You need to communicate with both the individuals and never assume who is the decision-maker until you are absolutely sure -- and even then, include the other people in the dialogue and don't ignore them.

Why? In many situations, the other person may be an influencer. It is said that women influence up to 85% of purchase decisions. Think about it for a second. The product or service may be exactly what you're looking for, but if the lady doesn't like the color of the product or doesn't like the salesperson, the decision-maker will have a difficult time pulling the trigger on the purchase.

This can also happen in business settings where you'll need to be dealing with the other person regularly even though they aren't the decision-maker. Again, the decision-maker will have a difficult time buying if the influencer is not comfortable with you or your products. Both of these individuals need to be on side.

Sales Is The Lifeblood Of Your Company

At the end of the day, if you make your living by being in business for yourself, you need to be able to sell. By default, this means devoting a certain amount of your time to sales. But what is enough time? This is always a difficult question, but if you have no business the answer is easy: 100% of your time. If you have some business but not enough, that number needs to be 60-80% until such time as the flow of orders starts coming. Then you can reduce the effort.

If, on the other hand, you have some form of recurring revenue stream but are still wearing many hats, you need to spend no less than 20% of your time on sales. The problem is most businesses have sales cycles. Some are natural while others are seasonal, and when we fill our order pipeline, we tend to shift our focus to execution and completely abandon sales. So in order to reduce or at least minimize the peaks and valleys, sales activity needs to be a continuous effort.

Educating Your Customers

The more your customers know about your business and how it works, the happier they will be and the more likely you will avoid any misunderstandings. David Ogilvy, a 20th Century marketing genius, frequently shared with his clients how to develop a great advertising campaign. His attitude was there was little risk in educating his customers about the business, as chances are none were going to go into the advertising business.

A customer that has been educated about your business will have a better understanding of why things need to be done a certain way. It has been my experience that many customers will make incorrect assumptions on how you should perform your assignment. As the expert, you have a duty to make sure the client understands why you do things in a certain way. Some will disagree with me on this and say the client only cares about the end result, to which I respond that this is a teaching moment. I find people appreciate learning something new. It also helps them to make informed decisions.

Everyone Is In Sales

Every single person that works in your company is in sales. Not just the customer-facing employees, but everyone. If they work for your company, they represent you and your organization. I'm not suggesting that you send your shipping clerk out on sales calls, but they do come in contact with your suppliers and, on occasion, your customers. To that end, how they handle themselves when interacting with these individuals will leave an impression. You need to make sure that the impression is a positive one.

How do they look? Does it reflect the image you want to portray? Are they polite and speak to these people in a respectful manner? Or are they gruff and impersonal? Take, for instance, your delivery people. Do they interact in a friendly manner with your customers? Are they knowledgeable about the products and services you offer?

Why is this important for sales? Well, there are a number of reasons. First off, if I use the example of a delivery person, they are the eyes and ears of your company. Let's say that they are on a regular delivery cycle. Chances are they interact more frequently with your customer than the salesperson. Let's further say that this person had a friendly disposition and had a great relationship with your customers. What do you think would happen if this individual were trained to be on the lookout for competing products being in your customer's place of business? Could they possibly suggest to the customer that they try your product the next time they order? Even if that isn't possible, they could at least refer the information back to the sales representative or the order desk.

Here's another example of why everyone is in sales. If you have employees, I suspect most of them commute to work. So what if you asked them to be on the lookout for new businesses opening up or even for existing businesses that could be potential customers while they make their way to and from work. Also, don't forget that non-sales personnel have friends and family that may just be in need of your products or services. Compound all this with the influence social media is having as people seek referrals and recommendations. You see, there are numerous opportunities for every one of your employees to positively affect sales for your company.

The point here isn't to turn everyone into full-blown sales representatives. It's to suggest that by hiring the right individuals and making sure they have a decent knowledge of the company, its products and services, everyone can help row the boat. Including all personnel in new product briefings will go a long way in making sure everyone is in sales.

4
Marketing

"If you're not telling anyone, you become your own best kept secret!"

-Greg Weatherdon

Would You Hire You?

Image is everything, and in business, it can mean the difference between success and failure.

As a purely hypothetical example, picture two landscaping businesses. One has employees who dress in clean, company-branded golf shirts, conduct themselves like professionals, provide detailed, written quotes upon request, have clean vans with the company logo on the side, and are consistent in their messaging when speaking with existing and potential clients.

Now contrast this with the employees of the second company that dress in a mish-mash of beer T-shirts and ripped jeans, scribble dollar figures on scraps of paper as quotes, haven't washed their beat-up vans in ages, use foul language while on the job, and bad-mouth not only their employer but past customers to existing and potential customers.

Which are you likely to hire? Both might provide the same service in the end, but in the case of the first company, image has been taken into account to show customers a highly-polished and professional organization from the first meeting. Because when you think about it for a second, with the company that puts that much effort into their image, there is a really good chance that they'll also care about delivering a quality product or service.

No matter what your business, your image is your first impression and your chance to get your foot in the door with prospective clients. There are no second first impressions, and if the first impression is poor, that will reflect on your business and the perception of your ability to provide good work.

It only takes on average 7 seconds for someone to form a first impression, and 93% of a first impression is based on how we look and sound.

It takes so little effort.

One Sight, One Sound

The most important element of a company image is that it's consistent in everything you do -- from the company logo on your employees' shirts to your business cards to your website. Everything done on behalf of the business should fit into that one consistent image. It provides a professional, customer-facing appearance that is attractive to potential customers.

Naturally, the image should fit the industry. That same landscaping company I mentioned earlier probably should not send employees out in three-piece suits, and business consultants should not approach clients in cargo shorts and flip-flops. Determine the image of your industry first, and then tweak it to differentiate yourself with your own image that people will learn to recognize. From its earliest days, long before it became a global giant, IBM demanded that all their sales people wore blue or dark suits, white shirts and conservative ties. It is rumored that that look helped to establish the company's informal name of "Big Blue."

Stretching that image across every facet of the business takes a lot of thought and some effort. Stepping back to look at your business with an objective eye, will help to discover the places where the image is not consistent. Business owners need to strive for that consistency, and one out-of-place element, such as the website design not matching business cards, can potentially create a disconnect in the eyes of your customers.

When I ran The Marketing Resource Group (MRG), I aimed to have a consistent image. The original company logo I designed was used on every piece of collateral material, including business cards, the website and every PowerPoint presentation we created. It provided a very consistent look to everything that was visible to the public. This may sound like a no-brainer, but thousands of businesses do not connect the dots when it comes to their image and just assume that their customers or prospective customers will figure it out --or worse -- that they don't care. That thinking is wrong. It does matter. So unless you're a graphic artist by profession or have a creative streak, you will want to invest in hiring a company to design your logo, business cards and all the other collateral material.

A very good example of a company with a very identifiable outfacing corporate image is Apple, which has a consistent look to its products and a corporate image that people can see from a distance. Take a look at an iPod, and compare it to an iPad, an iPhone and a Mac computer. Then contrast the products to the advertising and marketing around Apple, as well as its stores and even the unique appearance of the late Steve Jobs. It's an image that everyone recognizes, and it's consistent!

Boost Your Marketing

The line between sales and marketing skills is blurred. As one leads into the other, there's no clear distinction between some sales and marketing activities. Marketing, however, is entirely about generating awareness of your business that leads to business prospects, customer inquiries and ultimately new business.

Most small and medium sized businesses can't afford to have a separate marketing department, let alone a marketing manager. The reality is that the majority of these businesses don't have any formal or informal marketing plan. The most common way marketing is handled in these organizations is just to task an individual with this duty as part of their job description, or the business owner simply assumes this role. Good or bad, this is how it's done in a lot of companies.

It's all well and good to have a dream of a thriving business with a great reputation in the community it serves, but if you're not telling anyone, you become your own best kept secret. There is absolutely no excuse for any business not to make noise about what they do in this day and age. The amount of free technology available today is simply outstanding and doesn't require an advanced degree, just a little seat time to get up to speed.

Allocate Resources

Because many of us aren't skilled in the art of marketing, we too frequently fail to allocate any resources to this area. Resources are defined as time, effort and money. Why? Well it's simple enough. Because we're so busy trying to run our companies, we gravitate to the things we know and understand. Add to that that everyone and his brother has an opinion on what you need to do, and rarely do you ever get the same opinion twice.

The exception to this is social media where the term is thrown around like a panacea to cure all our problems. To the uninitiated, social media is just another black box of lotions and potions that simply adds to the confusion.

At the end of the day, if your target market doesn't know about you, you need to spend some time and effort -- and a little money -- to get your message out.

Business Cards

It's amazing how many businesses don't have what I would consider the bare necessities for marketing a business. I've met many small business owners that didn't have business cards, or if they do, they never carry them. If you have cards, they should be on your person at all times. If you don't have any, get some. Put extras in your bag, your car, your wallet and even give some to your significant other to keep just for added insurance. You never know when an opportunity may arise, and having this little piece of collateral could just make a difference.

Domain Name

For the cost of two lattés, you can register your company domain name. If you haven't done so, make sure you absolutely try to get the .com top-level domain. Regardless what everyone is saying about the new domain extensions, .com is the standard and will be for awhile yet. Failing that, at least try to get your country top-level domain.

Website

No excuse here either. There are so many low or no cost options available, it makes no sense to me why companies don't have an Internet presence. It is estimated that 50% of businesses don't have a website.

Don't think a website is important? Think about this for a second. Generation Y, those born between 1982 and 2004, currently outnumbers the Baby Boomers. Why is this cohort important? Chances are they are either your current customers or soon will be. Ask them when was the last time they read a newspaper and you may be shocked that their answer may be not in days, weeks or months, but possibly years. Ask them when was the last time they opened a phone book and you may get answers that range from "what is a phonebook?" to "I can't remember." Not convinced yet? When was the last time **you** looked up a number in the phone book?

Why do you think newspapers around the world are failing? Generation Y is not buying them. They get their news and information via the Internet. So if you're not there, you are invisible to this very large cohort.

At the very least, put up a basic splash page that shows you exist. Make sure you include your contact information. Want to move up to a low cost solution? Most of the blogging software available today has morphed into pretty decent and flexible website software. However, if you can afford it, hire a professional web firm to design a site for you and get visible.

Email

I'll admit that this is a pet peeve of mine, but it's all about continuity and consistency. Nothing says "amateur hour" like having a gmail.com, yahoo.com, etc. account listed on your business card, website or on the side of your vehicle. It's even worse when you're promoting a professional services business or dealing with large corporations. Again, this is all about image. If you want to play with the big companies, you need to act like one. You don't have to like it, just accept it.

The cost to have email on your domain is minimal, so there really is no excuse. I know, you like having the flexibility of web-based email because it's available anywhere and you don't have to manage it. It's a moot point, because most packages include webmail. But if you're looking for a truly low cost alternative, Google will host your domain email for about $50/yr.

Not everyone will buy into this concept, and that's okay. I actually know a few very successful individuals that do not use email on their domain and use only Gmail email. The difference between them and us is that they are very well-known, and people go out of their way to contact them because they want what they offer. It works for them, but not for most.

My last thought on email is that you should use the signature option that is available on most email software. Aside from your basic contact information, you can also use it to promote a new product or service you're offering, or depending on your business, it could be your weekly specials. If nothing else, it should have your website, social media links and your company tagline. Whatever you do, keep it simple and clean so that it isn't perceived as hardcore advertising that will annoy the recipients. Aside from a little effort, this is a no cost tactic that anybody can use.

Guerilla Marketing

There are books aplenty on guerilla marketing and low-cost marketing methods you can use to promote your business. As with sales and everything else you need to learn about running your own business, take a look at a few books on marketing or listen to audio books on how to effectively market your business.

Guerilla marketing may sound hokey, but in some ways, it's more effective than many methods that have been used in the past -- and it lets you get more creative, especially if money is tight. Think about how often you use some of the promotional items you receive from companies. Do you ever wear their T-shirts?

Here are a few low- or no-cost ideas you can use in your marketing strategy:

Newsletters

A regular newsletter that goes out by email, supplemented by the occasional traditional mailings, will establish a communication route between you, your customers, business partners and suppliers. I recommend sending out at least the occasional newsletter by mail because of the inherent problems of email. Email newsletters have this awful habit of ending up in spam folders or getting deleted without ever being opened.

Mail, on the other hand, has a fairly high recall rate because people get so little mail these days that isn't bills. Flyers that tend to be mass-delivered only get looked it, if at all, if someone has an immediate need. They have little recall potential and usually end up in the recycling bin. This kind of communication is more of a shotgun approach to marketing versus a targeted newsletter.

Even a handwritten note thanking a customer for their business or inviting a prospect to a special business function goes a long way towards keeping your name in the forefront.

Special Events

When I was younger, car dealerships had special unveilings for the next year's models. Only special customers got an invite to what was a rather prestigious event.

Although there are no surprises like that in the automotive manufacturing world any more, you can still hold special events for your best customers. Events can run the entire range of costs -- from low-cost gatherings to high-cost arena box rentals. Consider how you might be able to run an event of interest to your customers while staying within your budget. A promotional event to clear out old inventory is one idea that will cost you very little, while also allowing you to get rid of inventory you've been sitting on and turn it back into cash all while limiting attendance to existing customers or potential prospects.

Invoices

Believe it or not, invoices can be used as a form of marketing, as well as a request for payment. Consider this: On the bottom of every invoice, write "please refer a customer to us" or "please tell a friend." Offer an incentive for referrals, and people are even more willing to help bring you new business. You can also use it to remind customers of other services you provide. You may think they know all about you, but you'd be surprised how little they know about all your services.

Referrals

As previously noted, don't be afraid to ask for referrals. With rare exceptions, people like to help others. Referrals are a huge part of marketing and lead generation strategies.

Marketing Collateral

Business cards, brochures, letterhead and all the other marketing collateral that help you market your business, really cost very little. They're vitally important not only in marketing, but also in creating the image of your company that customers and prospects see.

Social Media

Facebook, Twitter and professional networking sites like LinkedIn have brought people together from all over the world. Businesses have found ways to use social media to communicate with their customers, partners and suppliers while generating new business.

Unfortunately, some businesses don't make good use of social media and forget it shortly after their pages go live. However, social media is shaping the lives of all generations, but in particular Generation Y, which is now in the workforce and expects the businesses they deal with to provide content and accessibility in the ways they themselves are communicating.

Learn the do's and don'ts of social media, and then use it as a tool in your marketing toolbox.

Networking

Get out there and meet people at events presented by your local chamber of commerce, small business associations and other key organizations. It costs little, but the visibility of being at events and supporting the communities will in turn help you find new business.

Also seek out the networking groups in your area and see which ones might be a fit for you. By fit, I mean that it fits your interests and is attended by your target market.

If you're not comfortable walking up to strangers and striking up a conversation, do a web search for tips and tricks. It gets a lot easier the more you do it. Believe me, I used to hate doing it, but now I have become quite comfortable in those environments.

Seminars

Why not host an information session or educational event that will serve to educate your existing clients about your products or services and how to use them? It can also be used to introduce potential customers to your company. You can even bring in a guest speaker to talk about a subject that would be of value to your customers.

Whatever you do, don't make it an infomercial or create a high pressure sales environment. Your objective is to provide value to your customers without them feeling any pressure to buy. They will look upon you and your business as someone who cares about them as customers.

Don't Follow The Herd

Using the same marketing techniques that everyone else in your industry is using won't help you to stand out. Think about how many fridge magnets you've received from real estate agents. Do you think that works as a marketing tool?

Think creatively. Think outside the box. And look for opportunities to do something unique. Have fun and be creative. People will remember you for it, and you just might be surprised with the results.

Get Your Business Online

Prior to the Internet, the Yellow Pages dominated our search functions, but now it is increasingly shrinking and disappearing from common vernacular. Now when people look for a product or service, the first place they go is online and increasingly via their smartphones. Just think for a moment, when was the last time you opened a paper-based directory?

Having a website with appropriate keywords regarding your business and location is critical to making it easy for potential customers to find you. It should also be designed to be consistent with your company's other marketing materials so as not to create confusion. Your logo should be front and center.

There's plenty of discussion about the need to have social media as part of a business marketing plan, but start with the website. Facebook pages, Twitter feeds and other social media marketing can come later. With the ease and affordability of getting a website built on WordPress, a common website design platform that is easy to learn to use, there are no excuses for not having a website.

Get Professional Help

If you're unsure how to improve your image -- or if you're someone who has a significant other who constantly remarks "are you really going to wear that?" -- seek professional help from the outside. There are expert image consultants, public relations people, marketing professionals and others who can help develop your image and put you on the right path.

Developing a good company image that fits with your industry will take time and effort on your part, but the rewards are greater than you may think.

5
Analyzing Your Business

**"True entrepreneurs have the
ability to see around corners."**

- Greg Weatherdon

Let me ask you: Do you really know what products or services you pro-vide generate the most revenue? Do you know what products or services generate the most profit? No WAGs (Wild Ass Guesses) here. Can you answer these questions with specific dollar amounts or percentages off the top of your head? If so, kudos to you; and by the way, you're in the minority.

It's all well and good to suggest that the business owner should focus on their area of expertise as well as those areas that deliver the highest margins and maximum revenue. But how do you do this?

Fortunately, it doesn't require an advanced degree or specialized training and can be achieved with nothing more than a pencil and paper, but realistically you'll want to break out the laptop and spreadsheet.

Most owners have never taken the time to thoroughly analyze their businesses from a revenue or profitability standpoint, so they don't have any idea what areas of their businesses are making them money. Always remember that "revenue is not profit, and profit is what pays the bills."

Whatever business you're in, unless you have organized your efforts and focused in on what really generates revenue and profit, you may be exerting effort for little reward. To make the most of a business and maximize its efficiency, the business owner needs to focus efforts on what the business is good at.

The best way to begin this process is to create a visual representation of your products and services in a practical way -- much the same way you have created a visual representation of your company's major roles and departments.

By organizing a business by product or service, you will get a better sense of the efforts that generate your company's revenue, the ones that generate your profit, and which are the mission-critical activities and core competencies of the business you have built. To determine what those mission-critical activities and core competencies are, ask yourself two fundamental questions about your business: What do you do better than others? What do you have that nobody else has?

Additionally, this exercise may help you uncover which areas of your business are sucking the life out of you and your company without compensating you enough for the hassle.

Step One: Getting Your Business Organized

Most business owners look at their company's revenue-generating activities as a bunch of different things they do, and over time, they find it difficult to explain exactly what they do to potential customers. They eventually start using generic terms like "we do landscaping" or "we run a bakery." Often, they make it more difficult than it needs to be, and the reason for that is they haven't organized their businesses and grouped like products and services together into lines of business.

At MRG, we had a variety of things we did for clients -- from retail telemarketing to broadcast fax to closed captioning of commercials. If we looked at each individual service on its own, it could be very difficult to explain what we did, but when we grouped the different activities into four key categories, it became very easy to look at the business model and give a high level overview of the entire business.

If you do, in fact, run a bakery, your product offering might look something like this:

However, if you group these same products into natural revenue pillars, it would probably look very much like this:

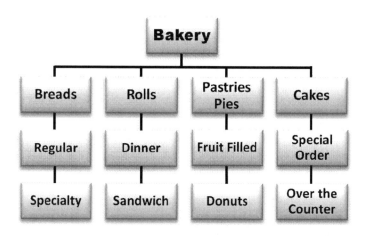

Every business has different revenue streams, and by organizing them, you'll find it's easier to present your business to customers, but it also gives you and your employees a much better idea of what your business does, where its revenue comes from, where profit comes from, which individual activities support others, and where best to spend your time and effort, and your advertising and promotion dollars.

MRG had four major revenue streams. We did retail telemarketing for the packaged goods industry, telemarketing for the pharmaceutical and healthcare industries, support services (such as direct mail and broadcast fax), and media services around creating broadcast television advertisements. When grouped, everyone at the company was better able to tailor their explanations of what we did to customers and break down individual service categories.

The organization chart I developed also showed me that although the first three categories of services were closely linked and supported each other, the media services had little to do with the rest of the company. With that in mind, I eventually spun off media services into its own company, which became MRG Media.

To get an idea of how to truly understand your business, break down all of the individual products or services your company offers and look for commonality. Group services into lines of business like the bakery example above. Just as large businesses have their revenue streams grouped into separate departments, so too can a small business do the same to gain greater understanding of the company and its services.

It will make it easier to present to customers what you do and what value you bring to the table, but more importantly, you'll be one step closer to managing your business instead of just working for your company.

Step Two: Analyzing Your Business

Organizing your business by departments only scratches the surface of truly understanding your business. After that, deep analysis is required. Unfortunately, there's no quick fix here, and it requires some grunt work to go through everything about your business. However, analyzing your business will be very enlightening.

To do this, you'll need:

- Revenue data by client. You'll either need to gather up all of your invoices or, to make it even easier on yourself, run a report from your accounting software.
- Input costs by client. You'll need to know labor and materials costs.

- A worksheet.
- Quiet time. It will take time to analyze your business, and you'll want to be largely undisturbed.
- Common sense. Once you have all the numbers and your business data, remember that the purpose is to get some analysis and insight into your business, its revenue streams and its profit margins. You'll have to look at your business from a practical standpoint and take your industry knowledge and challenge it against the numbers you see on the worksheet.
- Do it once, do it right! Stick to it until you've completed it. You'll be glad you took the time and finished this exercise.

By taking all of your invoices or your accounting software, you will be able to figure out by client and by product and service what revenue was actually earned and from where. Set up income by category. Then run the numbers to figure out the costs for each client, product and service to do some margin analysis.

It will take quite a lot of time, but at the end of the process, you will know exactly where your revenues come from and which clients, products and services are profitable -- and by how much. Once you've completed this exercise, be on the lookout for a pattern of missed cross-selling opportunities. These sometimes minor missed opportunities can greatly enhance your profitability on an order or project.

Know When to Hold 'Em

As I mentioned earlier, every entrepreneur wants to be all things to all people, and many of them don't want to say "no" when a client asks for a particular service, whether the business offers it or not. What typically happens, and I hope becomes evident, is that after a few years, you'll be offering services that may or may not fit into your business model and may or may not be profitable.

After you've completed the analysis of your business, you'll need to keep that practical mindset and look carefully at each business. Here are some questions you need to ask:

- Are you generating enough ongoing revenue to justify keeping it as a service offering?
- If so, is it generating sufficient profit margin?
- If not, can it be improved quickly so that it does?

If a product or service is earning you 65% margin, then great; but if it's only earning you 15% margin, you need to question whether it's worth holding on to. It may be better to take the resources you're using for that low-margin service and put them towards higher-margin services. Simply put, using this example, if you assume your costs/expenses are the same for the 65% margin product and the 15% margin product, it means that for every dollar of effort you can either make 15¢ or 65¢. Where do you think you should be concentrating your efforts?

There is no simple answer when it comes to deciding which products or services are worth keeping and which ones to terminate. You'll need to look at each element of your business and decide for yourself if offering a particular service is worth it. In some cases, a low-margin service may be intertwined with a higher-margin service that customers order together.

A typical example of this would be in the upholstery business. This business is fairly competitive, so pricing is important and margins are always under pressure. One way upholsterers increase their profit on a job is to offer a spray-on fabric protector that they buy in bulk. The cost to you is approximately $100; their cost is $10! Add a little labor and their margin is about 75%. A combination like this could increase their profitability by an additional 25%.

Be practical. Look at your core competencies. Use your common sense. If you can't gain critical mass on a service or you simply can't develop the industry expertise to be really good at it, don't be afraid to terminate that service category. Alternately, consider outsourcing that particular service to a trusted partner who may have the expertise and volume to be profitable providing this service. There is one question you can ask yourself that might help in making your decision: If I was starting the business today, would I want to offer this service?

Why Do This?

Learning to understand your business takes a lot of time, effort and work, so why would you do it when you could instead be out gaining new business or serving existing customers?

Getting a good understanding of your business gives you the knowledge you need to focus on profitable products, services and customers. When you've narrowed your business to what you're good at and what is profitable you'll have simplified your business, allowing you to enjoy what you're doing.

The curse of the entrepreneur is that if a client asks for something the business doesn't do, that service suddenly becomes something the business begins offering. It's not easy to say "no" to a customer, but some of these add-on services are totally out of the business owner's element and often end up costing more money, time and effort than it's worth.

Remember that you're trying to develop a better lifestyle and have your business work for you. And more often than not, less is more!

The following quote from Antoine de Saint Exupery is a great reminder of why we should look for ways to simplify and focus our businesses:

"Perfection is achieved not when there is nothing more to add, but when there is nothing left to take away."

Understanding Your Customers

Once you have a greater understanding of your business, you should have a better idea of where your revenue and profit are coming from, as well as who are your most important customers. Although a lot of small business owners start out by thinking that everyone is a potential customer, the truth is your ideal customer will fit a specific mould.

Just as your business has its core competencies, and as you have uncovered in the last couple of chapters, that some products and services are far more profitable than others, the same thinking applies to your customers. Just like your products and services, some customers are more profitable than others.

The reasons for this vary from geographic location to industry type to the services you provide to them. So the purpose of understanding your customer is to help you identify the characteristics of your ideal customer. Why? Figuring out the profile of your ideal customer is important because once you know who your ideal customer is, you can focus all your company's sales and marketing activities on attracting more of these ideal customers to your business. The technical term for this exercise is "profiling."

When I started MRG, the typical customer I dealt with was senior management, predominantly male and had certain predictable interests and career backgrounds. For example, most of them were golfers and had made their way up through the ranks of either the sales or marketing areas of their organizations from very junior positions. So for instance, enhancing existing relationships may include inviting the individual out for a round of golf.

The interesting thing was when we undertook this segmentation of our customers, we quickly realized that a paradigm shift started to occur. Where middle and senior management was once almost entirely male, many of these positions were now being held by females. Fortunately, this analysis helped us to get out in front of this change and allowed us to begin altering our approach and messaging to these individuals because they had different interests and a different way of doing business than their predecessors. In other words, golf may not be the best vehicle to enhance relationships with this group of people.

As I've said before, as small business owners, we like to think that everybody is our customer, but the net result is your most profitable and biggest customers could be, for example, "dual income families with young kids, living in the suburbs, who have just purchased their first home."

If that's the case, you need to now figure out the best way to narrow your marketing activities so that you're targeting this prime customer group.

The old saying that "birds of a feather flock together" is quite appropriate when targeting a specific demographic because like-minded people tend to have the same value system and enjoy the same kinds of activities. So the questions then become, "where do young families with kids hang out? How can I effectively reach them with my marketing message?"

This may not be as daunting a task as you may think. If you happen to fit your customer profile, where do you hang out? What do you read? Don't fit the profile? You can turn to your friends and family that do fit and get their input. Identifying your ideal customer allows you to be highly efficient in your marketing activities.

Gather Customer Information

While collecting data to get an understanding of your business, you should also get information about your customer -- gender, age, location or even special circumstances under which they tend to purchase your product or service, etc. If this is not the kind of information you've been collecting, I suggest you now incorporate it into your daily activities. It doesn't need to be a detailed study on each customer, but knowing a few key pieces of information will help you later generate a profile of your average customer. For instance, if you run a landscaping company, it would make sense to record the gender, approximate age, marital status, number of children (if applicable), size of household, location and, if possible, what kind of work they do. Your ultimate goal is to garner some insight into what tends to trigger the "need" and hence the "purchase."

If you don't currently have this information, you'll need to make an educated guess about each of your current customers. Once this is completed, you can now compare and hopefully confirm it against the information you're now capturing.

Analyze Your Customers

There's a science to profile analysis, but in determining the typical traits of your customer base, you don't need to be that detailed. As a small business owner, what you're looking for are similarities between your customers.

By examining the customer data you have collected, you'll be able to paint a picture of your ideal customer and learn where the majority of your business is coming from. You'll not only get a basic profile analysis of your customers, but by going through the process, you will also learn about the geographic location of your customers.

If you own a landscaping company, and as the picture of your customer starts to come together, you may discover that your largest profit center is with middle-aged married couples with large homes in the city that call on you for repeat work, or alternately, it's in townhouses owned by busy, young professionals that call on you regularly to do small jobs.

The largest profit center may also be in the city, even though you find yourself traveling to the suburbs for jobs on occasion. Identifying this key geographic area may help you to streamline your organization and increase your company's efficiency. Additionally, tightening up your geographic area can also generate higher visibility and to gain critical mass, which also drives efficiencies.

The same thinking applies if you provide consulting or professional services. By targeting a specific industry, you become far more visible within that industry and become the perceived solutions expert. Knowing what your customer profile is will help you target your marketing and sales efforts.

Unlike the hard numbers of analyzing your business, analyzing your customers will be more subjective. It will require you to develop a consistent way of keeping track of data so you can continue to gain insight into your most profitable customers. Even if the profile you come up with seems like it's not very specific, it's better than the wild-assed guess you would have been making prior to collecting and analyzing this data. Over time, you should be able to accumulate enough information so that the picture of your ideal client becomes clearer.

Don't Forget, Things Change

Throughout the life of your business, your customers may go through changes that you would otherwise not know about if you weren't keeping details on your customers.

People prefer to do business with people they like and trust and will also refer them to others. What frequently happens in small businesses is that as the years go by, your customer base doesn't change insofar as the names, but the demographics change. The young professionals living in urban townhouses become middle-aged people with families in the suburbs before becoming senior citizens with grandchildren.

Small business owners have to make choices about their customers. Many go with the flow of their changing customer base. Alternately, others focus on an individual market segment and see their customers turn over entirely every so many years.

There's no right or wrong answer, but knowing how your customer profiles are shifting will help you plan accordingly. Armed with this information, you can be more focused and stay closer to some of your customers. Remember, it costs 5-10 times as much to gain a new customer as it does to keep an existing customer.

Taking the time to do the heavy lifting this analysis requires will be well worth the effort. Not only will it help you to identify your most profitable customers and geographic areas, it may well serve to identify up-and-coming opportunities.

Too often we take for granted that we really know our customers, but by doing this analysis on a regular basis, it serves to validate our assumptions or give us a reality check.

6
You

**"Step out of your comfort
zone and grow."**

- Greg Weatherdon

Trust Your Instincts

Time and time again I see people getting advice from all the wrong people. It's okay to ask your friends for their opinions on something, but make sure you ultimately get professional advice on the subject.

Using the information you gathered from friends and family will help you to better understand something, but take it for what it's worth. For the best advice, go to a professional. It may cost a little, but most times, free advice is worth about as much as you paid for it. So if you need accounting advice, talk to an accountant.

Getting the right advice is only half the battle, as it has been my experience that the information you receive usually has options, so at the end of the day you're still left with making a decision. And this is where the fun starts.

For many of us, serious decision-making is not always an easy thing to do. How can it be? We've never received any training. Many times, we are left with only a feeling as to what is the right decision, and even then the right choice is rarely clear-cut. And just to complicate things even more, the right decision is probably not the coolest or the most fun, but it is most likely the best.

What I have found as one of the best things you can do to solve this dilemma is to listen to your inner voice.

What's that, you ask? Many refer to it as their intuition, others call it their conscience and still others call it their instincts. It's what Yoda of Star Wars fame refers to as "The Force." That voice -- or whatever we call it -- is usually very perceptive and, for the most part, very accurate. In its own little way, it has managed to capture and distill all of your life experiences and learnings.

Carl Jung, a renowned Swiss psychiatrist, said that a person in whom intuition was dominant, an "intuitive type," acted not on the basis of rational judgment, but on sheer intensity of perception. In other words, our intuition has somehow kept track of all the right choices we've made, as well as all the wrong decisions, so that every time we are faced with a decision or choice, it processes all those past experiences for us and tries to let us know which choice we should be making. How many times have we said "I should have trusted my instincts?"

The problem is most of us have ignored it for so long that we probably don't even hear it any more. The good news is that it is always there; we just have to learn to listen for it and recognize its signals. It's not 100% right, 100%

of the time, but as you make more and more decisions and learn to pay attention to it, you'll find that it becomes easier to make that right choice and trust The Force.

As entrepreneurs, we are faced with making many decisions a day, so it's in our best interest to develop every tool at our disposal.

We don't get training in making decisions or how to use our gut or how to build instincts. We learn these by adding experiences to ourselves, which go into our toolbox that we pull out to use when we need them.

May The Force be with you!

Think Big, Act Big (But Staying Small Is Okay)

Some business owners think that if they aren't growing their businesses, they're not succeeding. Don't buy into that. If you want to grow your business into a global concern, that's perfectly fine and I wish you luck. However, if you want to maintain a certain size of business, whatever that may be, there is absolutely nothing wrong with that. Not every business needs to be a multi-billion dollar global enterprise -- and most won't be. In fact, 90% of businesses in the Western world are classified as small- or medium-sized businesses. It's what many of these economies run on.

So for those of us who won't be building an empire, we can learn a few lessons from the big guys to make our businesses more presentable to potential customers and buyers. If you recall the two organization charts from a previous chapter, this is the jumping off point to get you started. Even if you only have five employees, by creating an organizational chart of all the roles within your company you will have a visual reference as to who is filling which role. The next step is to officially assign the tasks to those roles. This will go a long way towards initiating operational efficiency.

Too often, the typical small business owner doesn't think about the business as having departments, roles within those departments, and tasks within those roles. Such owners may say they don't have a sales or customer service department, but they do. It may be one person but that one person is responsible for multiple roles, and every business -- no matter the size -- has departments that can be organized properly in an organization chart.

Give employees the responsibilities and guidance, make sure they understand that you're available should they require clarification, and then step back and get out of their way. Just like any coach of a sports team, they train their players, but they aren't on the field running the plays. The most successful large businesses aren't micro-managed from the top down, and neither should smaller businesses be run that way. Not if they want to succeed, that is.

Remember the old adage that people want to deal with successful people. Look successful, act successful, be successful.

Cash Flow

Unless you have a high gross margin business that affords you a plump bank account, the bigger your company, the bigger the bills and the greater the demand will be placed on your cash flow. If you stop and think about it for a second, you'll need more employees to do more work, and that means a significant increase in your payroll. Overhead and operating expenses will also increase because you'll need a larger office or facility just to house your expanded workforce. All these items put a strain on cash flow.

If cash flow is already a problem for your business, as it is for many of us, then creating more expenses isn't going to solve the problem. It will, however, make it worse.

If you think about how much money it takes to get a business started, consider that it will take an equal amount of money to grow the business because you will be continually reinvesting the profits back into your company. Return on equity or return on capital are all great yardsticks to measure a business' progress, but never lose sight of the need to have sufficient cash available to get you through a challenging period. If you spend it, you've just pulled the safety net out from under yourself.

Keep in mind that you must build for capacity, which means that in many cases you're going to be incurring higher expenses before generating the required revenue to support the added costs.

Facilities

This won't be a problem if everyone telecommutes or lives offshore, but that's rarely the case. More employees, more inventory and even more office stationery requires more space. Continually growing businesses will be faced with finding and outfitting physical space. It sounds exciting, but in reality it can be quite stressful and expensive.

Additionally, if you're in a low-margin business, taking on more space may not be affordable. Finding enough space that fits into your expenses may prove challenging -- or even impossible. Again, when in empire building mode, you are going to be looking at physical space that will serve your long term needs and therefore you'll be taking on more space and costs than you currently need.

Employees

More employees beget more employees. The larger you grow, the greater number of supervisors and managers you'll require to oversee and train the new recruits. The process of hiring is not an easy one, and when you're rushed to continue growing your employee base, mistakes tend to get made.

If you keep growing, you will have to add new employees to your staff on an ongoing basis, and you'll need to find staff that fits your culture. The more employees you bring on board, the more your corporate culture is put at risk of being changed. Where people were once part of a small, happy team, they'll become increasingly unhappy and start complaining. Don't make the mistake of thinking you're immune to this behavior; it happens in every company that grows.

Also keep in mind the old (and very true) adage that two employees together are talking about the boss, three employees are talking about the company and four employees are starting their own company. It's another cliché, but it's a truism in business.

Clients

The bigger your business becomes, the more you have to ensure that you not only maintain your service levels but somehow also maintain the constant need to focus on new client acquisition. As your expenses increase, so too does your need to increase your revenue by at least as much.

That's not to say you can stop looking for new customers or sales opportunities. It's more about deciding how much growth you want. Without adding new customers or revenues, inflation alone will destroy your profitability as the costs associated with running your business will increase every year. In addition, sourcing new clients as every business faces client turnover. So for these two reasons alone you need to keep your business growing at 5-10% a year.

The point is that a small business can maintain service levels a lot easier than many large businesses. Chasing new clients without considering how it will impact you, the business owner, just doesn't make sense. Make sure it's what you really want.

Freedom

If you feel you're working too hard now, building an empire is going to consume a far greater portion of whatever free time you have left.

Your 50-hour week may creep into 60 or 70 hours, and you will find yourself chained to your desk more often than you might want.

Define Your Success

The point here is that you define your success -- not industry pundits, nor other business owners. Not even me. As the owner of the business, you have the luxury and the responsibility of defining your own success.

Believe me, I'm not against trying to build an empire. I tried to do it and found out it wasn't for me. I found I was much more satisfied and discovered more enjoyment in running a much smaller enterprise. It was a choice I made because I could.

If you decide to strive for the greatness of a business empire, just make sure it's what you want to do and not something you feel you should do.

Be Curious, Be Forever Curious

Never stop learning: although this should apply to everyone, it is even more important for a business owner. The rationale is fairly straightforward. Regardless of what you think, what you don't know about running a business far exceeds what you do know.

Let me explain. When business owners first start out, they do so because they feel they are technically competent or have a degree of expertise in a specific area. That expertise may be in any of the numerous disciplines required to run a business such as sales or marketing or production or design, etc. Having some form of expertise is critical and that expertise is usually the genesis for venturing out on your own in the first place. Unfortunately, many assume that this single expertise is sufficient to allow them to run an enterprise. The reality is many are not skilled business people, just skilled talent -- and that just doesn't cut it.

If money wasn't a concern, the new business owner should, from the onset, hire people to fill all the roles in their company that they don't have the skills for, but unfortunately, reality dictates otherwise. That reality is the lack of funds to spend on anything but the basics as you begin your venture, and therefore you are required to fill all the roles to the best of your ability. For most of us, it's not a hardship, as the enthusiasm of starting your business keeps us motivated long into the nights.

However, after a few years in start-up mode running through the forest at break-neck speed, you should be at the point where you can settle down and relax a little, but again, reality rears its ugly head. You see, just as you think you've got a handle on how things work, the rules change. Maybe it's a new technology that threatens to disrupt your industry. Maybe it's new legislation that restricts what your employees can do or, God forbid, a new competitor has figured out a way to provide your service more efficiently.

The point is, nothing is constant in business. Just think of the impact the Internet had on the world. Client contact changed from face-to-face interaction or via the telephone to now where it's mostly electronic. Newspapers, where titans once ruled, are now crashing down around us as people source their information online.

So what's my point? You can't stand still and assume that things will stay the way they are. As a business owner you need to develop a learning attitude. This isn't something you can do occasionally, like checking the air in your tires; it needs to be a daily activity, an attitude, a habit. And once it has become something that you just naturally do, only then can you instill that sense of learning into your employees, because at the end of the day, they are the ones that are going to make your dreams come true.

So what do I mean by learning? Although formal classroom learning would be helpful, it does consume a lot of your time. Time you probably don't have. But that doesn't mean there are no alternatives. As a matter of fact, there is an overwhelming amount of information available to everyone at little or no cost and should fit easily into your day. The following is a list of free or minimal cost sources for learning that you should investigate.

Library

Many libraries provide a vast resource of free information for the business owner. You may think libraries are from a bygone era but surprisingly many are firmly planted in the digital age and are providing their customers access to electronic resources most businesses couldn't or wouldn't afford. In addition, they offer several sponsor-free seminar sessions on a variety of business topics.

Chamber of Commerce

Investigate your local Chamber and you'll find that many run educational events that cover every imaginable topic you need to improve your business. Many are breakfast or lunch sessions whereby subject experts present to the membership. These events are free or very low cost as part of your membership. Non-members usually pay a slightly higher cost. The additional benefit of these sessions is that they usually provide for a networking opportunity before or after the session.

Podcasts/Audio books

How much time do you spend in traffic? Aside from grumbling about it, how do you pass your time? Listening to the radio? Talking on your cell phone? What if you took that time to expand your knowledge on a subject? Podcasts are free and range from 15 minutes to one hour, and cover an incredibly wide range of subject matter. Not all podcasts are created equal, so some preliminary testing on your part will be required, but there are some wonderfully talented people sharing their knowledge. Find a topic of interest on the Internet, download the episodes to your portable media player or burn a CD and your vehicle now becomes a rolling university. They're also great to listen to at the gym. Audio books, on the other hand, are available for purchase online or in some cases, available for loan from your library. One book can provide you with many hours of information on a single subject.

Blogs

Another source of free information. Again, a little homework is required to ferret out those that offer true value versus those that are nothing more than infomercials. Fortunately, most blog owners are looking to provide valuable information to their readers. Although not as portable as podcasts, many blogs can be downloaded to an electronic device for future reading. I like to have available a variety of electronic articles to read so when I've got some downtime, like waiting for an appointment or having lunch, I can catch up.

Webinars

Free webinars are offered daily on a wide range of business topics and typically last less than an hour. The advantage of a webinar is that it combines audio and visuals to reinforce a point or show a product, and most webinars offer participants the opportunity to ask questions at the end of the formal presentation. As with podcasts, the quality and the motivation of the presenters vary, but you usually do walk away with new knowledge on a topic. There are a couple of negatives with webinars; you need to be at a computer to view it, and some are strictly infomercials with no practical information. On the other hand, you can just leave if you sense that's the case or find the session is not for you.

These are just some of my favorites, but the list of options is quite extensive. From books and magazines to paying to see an expert speaker seminar, there are more than enough options to satisfy everyone and no excuse for not trying to improve your knowledge in any area of your business.

As the owner of any business, you need to learn or improve on those vital skills that will keep your business moving forward and allow it to grow. What worked for you up and until this point probably won't carry you to the next level. And believe me, there are always skills that need improvement when you run your own business.

When speaking with other business owners, I stress that there should be a continuing desire for learning. An investment in learning is never a wasted investment.

My personal motto helps to remind me that I should be constantly learning new things and improving my skills. That motto is: "Be curious. Be forever curious." It has helped to keep me on track and remind me that learning doesn't end when that last school bell sounds.

Your Health and Well-Being

The old saying that "If you don't have your health, what have you got?" really should be taped to every entrepreneur's bathroom mirror. You see, regardless of what you think or what you have been told, being self-employed is a 24/7, 365-day a year job. Even on those days where you may not be actively doing something, your mind will be busily looking for ways to remind you about something, anything to ruin your utopic moment and get you thinking about business.

Now, to be honest, I have solved many problems and have come up with some of my best ideas, when I was not "technically" working. But if you're wondering if there is any hope for a future where you're not worrying or thinking about your business, the simple answer is, no! Talk to anyone who has a sustainable business and they'll tell you the same thing. At best, you will be able to tame the mental beast and keep it caged for extended periods of time, but it always manages to find its way back into your consciousness.

Running your own enterprise can be all consuming and can take a toll on your mental, emotional and physical well-being. Human you are, invincible you're not! Too often, we use the excuse that we're far too busy to take time out of our busy day to exercise or eat right or just go for a walk.

Time for Change

This may sound repetitive, and that's because it is, but if you made it through the start-up phase of your business, it's time to start making changes in what you do. As I've said before, during start-up it's necessary for you to wear many hats as your business transitions from an idea to reality. This hands-on approach is necessary because you're constantly making course corrections as your company unfolds, and the rush and excitement of your mission keeps you motivated. But as your company grows, the demands on your time also grow and what was an adrenaline-driven motivator can easily become a stress-induced existence. Is this what you signed up for when you first went into business?

When you first started out, it was understood that your life would be disrupted. It was justified under the guise of the price you have to pay to be your own boss, with the promise that things would get better once you got the business up and running. So has it? Sure, you may be making more money, but is the business still controlling your life? So again I ask, is this really what you signed up for when you started your company?

I'm sure you're thinking to yourself that you can handle it or maybe once you get that next big project or assignment, that will take the pressure off. Probably the same things you've been telling yourself and your family ... for awhile now. The thing is, if you seriously don't start to make changes in how you manage your business, you'll be singing that same song next year and the year after that, because there is always another project or contract that will set you free. What you forget is that once the thrill of landing that new piece of business has faded, the added workload brought on by the new client or project just adds to your stress level. What we don't see happening is that after prolonged periods of stress, the joy of running our business decreases ever so slightly. One sign that you need to be aware of is when going to work starts becoming a chore. If you're feeling this way even occasionally, it's time to make some changes before you become too cynical or apathetic about your business, customers and employees to care. These two emotions are some of the most destructive business forces around.

You're Not Supposed To Be The

Hardest Working Person In Your Company

Reread this heading. I know many owners who feel like they're the hardest working person in their companies, and what scares me is that many of them are proud of it. It's like a badge of honor that they proudly wear for all to see. They didn't start out with this being their goal; it just sort of happened either because they still think they're in start-up mode or they're just afraid of letting go.

If you're going to have any hope of getting out from underneath your business and begin to have anything that remotely resembles a normal life, you need to change your focus from one of doing to one of managing. Shear force of your will may help you achieve your business goals but probably does little for your personal goals.

You're probably thinking that you can't possibly deal with your personal goals when you haven't achieved your business goals. Wrong! You're the boss, and you can do whatever you want to do. Why is it that as entrepreneurs, we forget that we control most situations and that we have the power to make decisions to change what we want, when we want? We are the ones that are supposed to be in control, yet more often than not we let external forces dictate our actions to the detriment of our health and general well-being.

Living right, eating healthy and exercising while minimizing your stress will help keep you healthy, both on a physical and emotional level. If the business is going to put you in the hospital or destroy personal relationships, then why are you doing it? To my way of thinking, that's far too high a price to pay for following your dream.

Find Free Time

Finding some free time for yourself is not as daunting a task as it may at first appear once you unwrap yourself from your imposed self-importance and realize that some things can wait just a wee bit longer. Take a hard look at all the things you "must do" today and ask yourself what would happen if two or three of those items didn't get done? Chances are the world wouldn't end, but more realistically, you're probably leaving a list of things undone every day, anyway, so all I'm saying is take control and decide what items are mission-critical today and leave the rest. Contrary to what you may think, not all those things are mission-critical. Quite to the contrary, most aren't!

Lopping off just a couple of those tasks on your to-do list probably gives you just enough time to go for a walk or run before heading into the office, instead of your caffeine-induced dash out the door in the morning. Maybe you could just spend a few minutes with your family in the morning as they start their day. I bet you haven't done that in awhile.

The thing is it's not hard to find the time if you want to. Over the years, I noticed that many health practitioners that I've met have arranged their work week to include one morning or afternoon a week that is completely theirs to do what they want, and is not business-related. A number of them are marathon runners, and they use the time to train. I personally took Monday afternoons off during the golf season and had a standing tee time with some friends for almost a 10-year period. And as time went on, I began taking Fridays off as well to do whatever I wanted.

Make Time To Think

A lot of business owners are so busy that they're always reacting and have not set aside the time to do nothing but think. As the owner, your job is to guide your business. After you've moved out of start-up mode, you should be thinking more strategically about your business and doing less and less of the day-to-day work.

You can't do everything at once. No matter how common the word "multitasking" has become in today's fast-moving world, nobody can really multitask. What we do instead is juggle priorities and do one thing at a time.

Setting aside time to think will help you to focus on the business and what needs to be done, and it will also give you some quiet time in which to reflect and lower your blood pressure. It is said that stress is a result of not having too many things to do, but never finishing anything. So use this time to figure out what are the three things that are driving you crazy today and then deal with them. Then just keep doing this every day, focusing on the things that you know need to be dealt with instead of putting them off. I'll guarantee you'll get better and faster at it, thereby allowing you to spend more time thinking strategically about your business once you get the tactical stuff handled. Oh, and as far as all the other stuff you're trying to do, you may find out much of it isn't worth doing in the first place.

Delegate, Delegate, Delegate

You've probably been told 1,000 times that you need to delegate. Delegating as many of the tasks you're now doing is the only way you are ever going to get out from underneath your business and start enjoying the freedom self-employment can give you.

Delegating doesn't need to be an all or nothing activity. By handing over even a small part of an assignment, project or task, it starts both you and your employees down the path of shared responsibility for the success of your organization. As the individuals gain proficiency and you get comfortable in sharing the load, everybody wins. The team members feel they are contributing and you're freeing yourself from tasks you probably shouldn't be doing, anyway.

This does not happen overnight, but is a process that evolves over time as your staff gets accustomed to their new responsibilities and you get comfortable doing it. Mistakes will happen, but like teaching someone to ride a bicycle, not everyone learns at the same pace. As you learn to get out of your own way, you'll not only be better able to focus your efforts on the things that are going to make your company better, but you'll have more time on your hands.

Control Your Work Habits

When I started The Marketing Resource Group, I made a conscious decision not to take work home with me, and I rarely broke this rule during the 17 years I owned the company. This was in direct contrast to how I worked for the eight years at my previous company. This step is usually something you can control. It may take you awhile to get accustomed to do it, but the end result is that you start to put some distance between your business life and your personal life.

Business owners are always juggling 20 different things at once, but if you don't get something done, figure out how to get it done through other people. As I said above, delegate, delegate, delegate.

Control Your Clients

There are business owners that are bound to disagree with me, but a client's urgency doesn't necessarily make it your urgency. Although you have to try to accommodate clients, if they have a problem, it doesn't necessarily mean it's your problem. Take it from me: It's okay to tell a client that you can't solve their problem in the timeframe they demand as long as you didn't previously agree to something.

I have found that most clients -- not all, mind you; just most -- are usually pretty reasonable. If you explain to your clients why you can't meet their timeline for a project, most will understand. Don't get me wrong, we would jump through hoops when the client had a real urgency. The thing is, their demands may only be a result of them finally making a decision and they want it completed as soon as possible so that they can check it off their to-do list. Others just never considered that their request would not give you enough time to properly complete the assignment. I'm not advocating turning away business but suggesting it never hurts to ask the client for an alternative timeline if it can streamline your production.

Sometimes it's just the simple things that can free up your time. A classic example that I ran into regularly is when a client asked for an 8 AM meeting that was on the opposite side of the city. Trying to get to a meeting at this time would require me leaving very early and waste an additional hour in traffic just to accommodate them. Where once I would have accepted the meeting, I began asking if it were possible to move the meeting to 10 AM, explaining to them that this way I could avoid the traffic. With the very rare exception, they were quite willing to do so. The reality is they hadn't even considered my travel time because many of them lived close to their place of employment and never thought about the traffic I would face. Most small business owners will try to make any client request work no matter the difficulty it poses, when sometimes all you have to do is ask.

I finally developed a standing rule that I don't do meetings before 10 AM and not after 2 PM, and definitely nothing on a Friday afternoon. Rarely did I have to change my rule. This whole concept may seem counter-intuitive to some, but once you begin controlling your clients' demands, you'll be better able to control your own day.

Exercise Regularly

Exercise will keep you fit, increasing your health and also giving you a release for any stress that may be building up. I also found that exercise was a great learning opportunity by putting on an audio series on a topic that I wanted to learn more about while going for a run. I also found that exercise could also be a great distraction from the day's business events that sometimes overwhelm us as owners. The time away from the business environment also gave me time to think.

Take a Vacation

When was the last time you took a vacation? If you answer "it's been awhile," then you need to re-evaluate your priorities and your reasons. I often hear owners saying that they can't take time off. When probed as to why, they regularly answer that they can't leave the business for that long.

The problem is that they have made themselves invaluable to the business and their employees and never delegated responsibility to others within their companies. Is this really what you promised yourself and your family when you set out on this enterprise? Most likely not. In order to gain their support or at least their understanding, you probably painted a lovely mental picture of a better life and more time to do things together. So how are you living up to your end of the bargain?

Vacation time doesn't need to be a five-star event. It just means taking time away from the business. As I said earlier, you'll never quiet the mental beast, but you can physically remove yourself from the business and just do something else. This is important for your own renewal. Separation from the business helps you to see the forest instead of just the trees. It also gives you the opportunity to evaluate your priorities and make sure the business is delivering on your needs. Sort of like a grown-up's time-out.

As soon as I was able, I started taking quarterly holidays for at least a week at a time and sometimes longer. I could do this because I had set my company up to serve my needs by delegating and trusting my employees to take care of the place.

Maintain A Healthy Paranoia

When you own a business, stress and worry is simply a part of your life. Still, there's good stress and bad stress. It's akin to the "fight or flight response" that is hardwired into our DNA. The good stress -- **fight** -- is the one that keeps you on your toes and concerned about the future of your company. The bad stress -- **flight** -- is the one that can have a significant impact on your mental, emotional and physical well-being. The latter is the one that keeps you awake at night worrying, whereas the former is the one that focuses your attention on the things you need to do to stay competitive and moving forward. It's what I call a healthy paranoia.

Every business owner needs to maintain a measure of healthy paranoia. This doesn't mean believing the world is out to get you. Rather, it means you have to assume that the status quo won't remain the status quo. In other words, don't get comfortable with where you are. It's simply being realistic and assuming that you'll be faced with unexpected events that could cause more bad stress.

Having a healthy paranoia gets you mentally prepared for when the wheels on the bus don't go 'round and 'round. It assumes you're going to be faced with a sales drought, an industry paradigm shift or the loss of an essential employee. A healthy paranoia keeps you hungry and on your toes.

Plan For The Worst

What would happen if you lost your largest customer? What would you do if a key employee decides to leave? It may sound incredibly negative, but you have to assume you're going to face a catastrophic loss at some point. Assuming that this will never happen is simply naïve. It's akin to sticking your head in the sand because you just don't want to think about the possibility of such an event.

For me, maintaining that level of healthy paranoia drove me to ensure that all my staff positions had a backup. Having employees that were cross-trained in each other's responsibilities assured me that in the event of illness or departure of any employee, the company wouldn't be effectively crippled. By doing so, this would allow us to continue operating and focused on maintaining high customer service levels while giving us breathing room until we could find a replacement. Fearing the worst means you plan for it in a calm and controlled manner. It's fear in a healthy manner.

And the worst will happen.

Hope For The Best

Healthy paranoia is a state of mind more than anything. Just when you think you've made it, something or somebody derails your plans. Knowing it could happen is exactly the attitude you need so that you are prepared for it and able to calmly manage the situation should it arise.

It's easy to turn healthy paranoia into negativity, though, and that's the wrong kind of attitude to have. It won't help anybody, least of all you. Don't be negative; be grounded, be realistic. Take a hard look at your business and determine which mission-critical activities, if disrupted, would seriously ruin your day. Do the same with your employees and your customers, and then devise ways to minimize the impact now. It's far better to plan for them when they're only a thought and not a reality.

Some business owners are overly pessimistic, whereas others are overly optimistic. A healthy paranoia will help you to keep a balanced perspective and ensure you have options when you face potential road blocks on the road to success.

Where's Your Wealth?

For newly-minted entrepreneurs, the biggest priority is to generate revenue, any revenue, in an effort to transition from struggling to profitable enterprise. For those of us who have made the crossing, we have more often than not sacrificed our own financial needs in order to create a proper fiscal foundation for our business. Because so few of us ever get investor capital, we are left to our own devices to fund our enterprises. That's okay. As that old saying goes: "What doesn't kill us makes us stronger."

Unfortunately, we have trouble letting go of this attitude once the business moves off life support and begins breathing on its own. Of course, this is understandable. Having lived through the tough times, it's not something we're eager to revisit. So under the guise of "reinvesting in the company," we continue to pour our profits back into the organization and rarely do we consider taking it out of the company. Not to spend on toys, but to take some risk off the table.

Considering most business owners hold upwards of 80% of their wealth in their business, this "all your eggs in one basket" scenario is a high risk situation. Ask these same owners if they would invest 80% of their net worth in shares of just one company on the stock exchange and they would certainly question your sanity. Yet these same individuals don't think twice about their current wealth strategy.

In my case, I had set a target of getting 66% or 2/3 of my wealth outside of my operating company and to provide for some creditor protection. I did this not because I was anticipating any sort of business crisis, but because I realized I didn't want all that I had worked for to be totally dependent on the future performance of me and my company.

Okay, so where and when do you begin? The following steps may help you frame your own initiative. Your corporate structure will dictate what vehicles are available to you and, by all means, consult your accountant, lawyer, financial planner and any other professional you need to maximize the effectiveness of any strategy you are considering.

1. Make sure you're taking a regular, dependable salary. Not your dream salary, but one that allows you to work without the stress of your personal financial situation overwhelming your decision-making. In other words, comfortably covering your basic needs.

2. Begin formally moving a set amount from your current account to your chosen vehicle, such as a holding company, corporate savings account, etc. The formula you choose can range from 5% of all your billings that automatically gets transferred monthly to upwards of 50% of annual profit being transitioned out.

3. This money should not be put at risk in another venture.

4. Although minimizing taxation is always important, it can't be the deciding factor.

5. Eventually you will have transferred at least a portion of your wealth and created another pillar in your financial portfolio.

If you were expecting some magic formula, I'm sorry to disappoint. This is basic wealth management, a rainy day fund, often ignored by business owners. Too many owners are hoping to cash in when they sell their companies and are devastated when they can't sell it or get significantly less than they anticipated and have no additional source of wealth.

Being an eternal optimist is a necessary ingredient to having any chance of success as an entrepreneur, but it needs to be tempered with a bit of realism. It's truly amazing the sense of freedom and security you feel when you've consciously created an additional source of wealth outside your operating company.

How you do it is up to you, but starting today in small increments is a must, because like a journey of a thousand miles, financial freedom begins with a single small step.

Do The Things You Enjoy!

With all the duties and responsibilities owners assume, it's of little wonder the burden of ownership burns out so many people. Of course, during start-up, it's all hands on deck. You do whatever needs to be done to get your business to a point where there is at least regular revenue in sufficient quantity to give you a degree of hope.

The next stage of evolution for every business can require just as much effort as getting your business off the ground. This is what I call the transition stage. This is the point in your company's life where many of the day-to-day operations **should** be happening with little or no input from you. I've bolded the word **should** because, unfortunately, letting go or delegating doesn't come naturally to many owners, and few actually make the transition.

The following saying sums up this transitory phase best: "Entrepreneurship is living a few years of your life like most people won't, so that you can spend the rest of your life like most people can't." Notice it doesn't say "Entrepreneurship is living your whole life." No, it says "a few years!"

And that's the whole point here. As your business matures, your focus should change along with your duties. Yes, it is critical that we are able to make the transition from no revenue to a functional, revenue-generating and profitable business. But it's equally as critical for you to delegate much of the work to others. This is the beginning point of where you are no longer working for the company, but the company starts to work for you. This is the point where you begin to free yourself up to spend more of your time thinking strategically about the business and also give you some freedom to focus on the things you really enjoy.

As the owner, you can never completely ignore any aspect of your business, but you can choose to focus your time on the things that make you happiest. If it's sales, then figure out how to spend more time selling. If it's marketing, then market. If you really like driving the forklift, then don't let anybody tell you it's not presidential enough; go work in the warehouse. It's your company and you can do whatever you want.

Let's be honest. As humans, we have a phenomenal ability to avoid doing the things we least enjoy. On top of that, when we do have to do them, we look upon the tasks as drudgery. Is this really the best use of your time or your creative energies? The answer is, probably not. At this transition stage you need to be delegating as many of these duties that you can so that you're able to focus on long-term activities that will help your company grow to a stable, self-propelled organization.

As a word of caution, delegating does not mean abdicating. After all, it's your business and your assets and you need to know how it's doing. You can keep abreast of what's going on by monitoring five or six objectives in every department and let your employees deal with the minutiae. As long as each department or area is running smoothly, you can maintain a high level overview. When there is a big problem, and there will be, the fact that you are now in control of your time allows you to roll up your sleeves and put your experience to work.

As the pieces begin to fall into place, you will begin to see how much more time you have. What you choose to do with that time is your decision. Want to work less? Then do so. It's your company and you don't need to ask permission. A small business owner's job is to manage the business. Otherwise, you're just another employee.

Seriously, you really need to consider how you're operating within your business. Ask yourself this question: Are you working for your company or is your company working for you? Only you know the real answer, but if it's the former, it's time for change. It's time to Get More Life Out Of Your Business!

7
Employees

**"Knowing exactly what you want
to achieve is the first step."**

- Greg Weatherdon

Trust Your Employees

After a few years running a start-up business, chances are you've become accustomed to wearing multiple hats and being directly involved in every aspect of your business. If you've done things right, you've surrounded yourself with good talent, but even so, many owners have a hard time giving up control and trusting their employees.

There are countless examples of small business owners 10, 15 or more years into their business who speak poorly about their employees and don't trust them to handle even the most basic of managerial and supervisory tasks.

They complain about their employees not taking initiative, not doing the job the way they want it done, and not being competent enough to be trusted with their "baby."

We've all made bad hires at times, but chances are most of your employees are good, hard-working people who want to take pride in their jobs -- and perhaps your own trust issues have made it impossible for them to rise to the challenges you'd like to give them.

Many small business owners never learn that "putting the fear of God" into their employees or yelling at them when mistakes are made is not the solution to their problems. If you want to make sure people stop taking initiative or responsibility, just start yelling at them or suggesting that they are lacking a certain mental horsepower when they make a mistake. It's pretty much a surefire way to shut them down.

Employees are people, and they want to be treated with respect, just as small business owners expect to be respected. Like a parent with a child pushing the boundaries of acceptability, give your employees room to make mistakes – very likely the same mistakes you made when you were first doing their job.

It has been my experience that mistakes usually occur because the employee was never given all the information -- and I mean **all** the information -- necessary to perform the requested task. If they make a mistake, a true manager focuses on resolving the problem and why it happened instead of focusing on the person. As the old saying goes, people learn more from their mistakes than they do from their successes.

Only when ample trust has been built up on both sides can you trust your employees to do what's in your company's best interests, even when you're not in the office. In fact, the beauty of being able to trust your employees is you'll get to a point where you can trust them to deal with disasters on their own without requiring your input.

For instance, when I ran The Marketing Resource Group (MRG), I built the company to be independent of me, and I trusted my instincts about people. While running MRG, I had achieved a great work-life balance and frequently was absent from the office. I trusted my employees to run the business in my absence, and I joked with them that they should only call me while I was on the road if there was a flood.

No one could have predicted that the subject of my jest would actually become a reality. While visiting Prague in the Czech Republic for my daughter's skating competition, I received a call from the office. The building had flooded. Standing in the middle of downtown Prague, thousands of kilometres away from MRG's headquarters, all I could do was ask a few key questions and trust my employees to solve the problem to the best of their abilities.

Not only did my staff not require me to fix the problem, from where I was physically standing in the world, I had no ability to do so. Although I was notified of the disaster, I trusted my staff to solve the problem, and they were up and running again quickly. They moved desks and office equipment, and the business was back to work within a day and able to meet the commitments we had made to our clients. By the time I returned, life in the office was returning to normal, albeit with a temporary new floor plan.

Trust your employees. They may surprise you. Whether a buyer comes calling or you finally decide to back away from the day-to-day operation, the ability of your staff can make or break the deal.

Developing A Culture of Learning

Learning doesn't stop with you, the owner. Quite frankly, it's the exact opposite. It's just the beginning. The big question then becomes: "Do you have a learning organization?"

I don't mean the traditional definition of a learning organization whereby you send people on industry or role-specific courses, or that you hire only individuals with significant post-secondary degrees.

My definition of a learning organization is nothing more than a business that encourages people to learn from each other and to openly share this knowledge throughout the course of their employment with your company.

When was the last time you shared an article of interest with your employees? When was the last time you shared a simple example of good or great customer service you received? It is said that we learn best from stories and less from theory, so it's in our best interest to make sure we share these real life examples.

Similarly, do you encourage your staff to share their knowledge with each other within your company, or is it a case of he who has the knowledge has the power? Just think for a moment how much more effective and efficient your company could be when knowledge is shared willingly and openly.

I'm really not sure who said it, but one of my favorite quotes is: "Every time you sit with an employee should be a teaching moment."

This is an incredibly powerful statement, and yet how many of us actually do this? I've found that the most enduring moments to put this into practice have been when an error or mistake has been made. Yet far too many times it becomes a wasted opportunity because we end up focused on trying to correct the behavior of the person that committed the error and not on learning what part of the process or system failed in the first place. It's just easier to assume the employee is at fault.

What if, once the crisis has been resolved, we then go on to engage the individual by sharing our knowledge on why it needs to be done a certain way, such as for regulatory or legal requirements, or where possible help them to make suggestions to correct the deficient process? Because if you think about it for a second, chances are they don't know why it needs to be done a particular way since they either didn't create the process or no one has ever told them.

Once you've shared your knowledge and helped them understand, they become far more valuable to the organization because you have helped them to grow their knowledge about your business or industry. Of course, all of this requires ongoing effort, so alternately, you could just walk away and tell them not to let it happen again, and miss the opportunity to create a learning organization.

Those truly dedicated staff will embrace these moments. And guess who benefits? Everyone! The employee benefits by feeling that their actions can make a difference to the company. The company benefits by having everyone focused on the same goals or objectives. And finally, you benefit by having engaged employees willing to follow you or watch your back because you've taken the time to be human and shared your ideas, thoughts or knowledge, and helped them become better and more confident.

One strategy that worked for me at The Marketing Resource Group was to put up a bookcase in an area accessible to everyone in the company (not my office) and fill it with books and audio series that I encouraged people to borrow to read or listen to.

Also critical is to keep an open mind and invite input from your staff. Many heads are better than one. Because your staff is engaged in the day-to-day activities of the company, they may already have solutions to problems. However, if they're not given the opportunity to have a voice, you may lose out on valuable knowledge and the chance for you to learn from those closest to you in your work life.

One last word on learning: Don't just do the easy stuff. Dig deep into subjects. One example of this is when I had heard about Dr. Deming's work on continuous improvement using statistical measurement. In a nutshell, this topic delves into measuring a process over a period of time, and then looks at ways to improve it. By continuing this cycle, you drive efficiencies into your company. Pretty deep stuff, but once I got into it, it became a fascinating topic and we began testing the theories. This also serves as an example of engaging your employees. I had one individual that worked for me that was particularly detailed-oriented, so I gave her the task of measuring existing information we already had and then tracking it forward. This individual embraced the topic and became our "expert."

If you nurture a learning environment from the top-down, your employees will take advantage of it, and your business will be better for it.

Hiring The Right Employees

Ask a dozen small business owners about hiring new employees, and you're likely to get a mix of reactions, from confusion to fear to outright disdain. With few exceptions, every business owner hates the hiring process -- not because they don't want to find the right employees to drive their businesses forward, but because hiring is an intensive, time-consuming and costly activity that they really don't understand.

Most business owners need to be a jack-of-all-trades for the first few years in their start-up phase. Most come to their business with some skills and quickly develop some degree of proficiency in those areas where they lack expertise. Getting up to speed on those weaker skill-sets is usually nothing more than the need to survive, and developing proficiency comes through repetition. Think sales, marketing and production, just to name a few. Because we're usually doing these tasks daily, we tend to get better at them.

Unfortunately for most of us, hiring is one of those skills that we don't use often enough to become proficient. The truth is, making a mistake in hiring is usually an expensive proposition that can affect your business in numerous ways, from destroying company morale, to losing customers, to seriously damaging your reputation.

Stop and think about it for a second. Unless you worked in a human resources department before starting your business, how often did you have to hire someone? I mean being solely responsible for every aspect of the process, from placing the ad, reviewing the resumes, interviewing the candidates, checking references, selecting the candidate, making an offer, negotiating details and finally processing all the necessary paperwork. Chances are most of us would answer "never" or, at best, "rarely."

If we were to be completely honest with ourselves, we'd readily admit that we're not very good at hiring. And why should we be? Most of us have never received any training, and we're simply going on instinct and make errors along the way, which occasionally results in the wrong employees being hired. Although you can't eliminate that possibility entirely, you can reduce your chances of hiring incorrectly by developing your own hiring practices.

Don't Panic

When it comes to hiring, the best advice I can give you is: Take a deep breath and don't panic.

There are only two reasons that you need to hire someone, but both bring with them a certain amount of stress, albeit for different reasons.

The situation that causes the most stress is when an existing employee decides to move on and only gives the minimum required notice. Of course, it only ever happens at the worst possible time. Depending on the size of your company, this could easily be a crisis situation in the making and, yes, highly stressful, because you might only have two weeks to find a replacement. Less, if you want the departing person to train the new hire.

The second situation is usually self-inflicted. This is when you're hiring for a new position because the company is expanding. I say "self-inflicted" because most business owners wait too long on hiring for that new position.

Far too often, the decision to hire is done when it is critical to get someone on board immediately. As business owners, we usually have a pretty good idea when our current human resources are at or near capacity, yet because of our prudent nature, we tend to wait far too long before we decide to hire the new person. At that point, everybody is maxed out running around trying to get the projects completed or shipments out the door. Everybody is working way too hard just trying to keep the customers you already have happy.

At this point, the whole hiring process usually becomes a rushed, ill-prepared venture with a higher than normal risk of failure. Had we hired when we first started to think about it, the process could have been a carefully planned and managed undertaking with minimum stress.

So why does it have to be this way? The simple answer is, it doesn't. But the real answer is that we tend to worry that the current growth in the business may not be sustainable. Therefore, we are not 100% sure that the business can support the added expense along with all the other imaginary what-ifs that cloud our thinking. The thing is you've probably mulled over all the ramifications of hiring or not hiring 100 times in your mind. You know the right answer, but fear of making a mistake is holding you back.

At the end of the day, much of this panic or stress can be also attributed to a lack of organization. What too frequently happens is that the hiring decision is made too quickly in a knee-jerk reaction to a situation. When this is the case, the odds of hiring the wrong person skyrocket.

One tip I can offer to increase the odds is that you should always be on the lookout for suitable candidates. For example, that pleasant counter server at the local coffee shop may have all the qualities you want for your next customer service person. Even if you can't hire them right away, make sure you get their contact information so you can contact them when you have an opening.

At the end of the day, you need to learn to trust your instincts and keep an eye on the horizon. By beginning the hiring process months before you'll actually need the new employee, you will hire better and make fewer mistakes. And remember, don't panic.

Develop A Hiring Process

Hiring is never a simple thing, and too often small business owners are ill-prepared for the role. Most owners really don't enjoy hiring because of the associated risks, but also because they don't know how to do it. Many think they do, but in reality they're not very good at it. Fortunately, there is a solution, and that is to create a hiring process to make hiring as simple, consistent and pain-free as possible to improve the odds of making a good hire.

Done once and done right, a hiring process put down in writing and taken out whenever it's time to bring on a new employee will make hiring easier and less stressful on you. Once in place, you won't have to reinvent the process or make it up as you go along; you'll have all the steps laid out for easy reference.

At The Marketing Resource Group, we developed a hiring process that was unique and designed to give the candidate a glimpse of our corporate culture all the while ensuring fairness and consistency between the candidates. It may not be the hiring process for everyone, but it worked for us and resulted in the hiring of good employees that understood what we stood for and expected.

So where do you begin in creating this hiring process? Well, before you do anything, you need to understand the position you're trying to fill. Focus not only on the job description that will later appear in job ads in newspapers and online, but on the traits somebody should possess if they were to be hired for the job. For instance, the receptionist you need to work the front desk and be the first face people see when they walk into your business should be friendly, well-groomed and good at dealing with people. This is in addition to being organized and able to manage incoming calls. Many businesses fail at hiring the right person for the receptionist's job. Think about it: How often have you gone to a company only to be greeted by someone who is gruff, abrupt and makes you feel like you're bothering them?

Just because someone has a shiny resume with all the skills you're looking for doesn't mean they have the personality traits you're looking for, so consider what it is you really need in an employee. If they're customer-facing. They need to be clean, personable, use appropriate language and always act in a professional manner. This also applies to your delivery person who is meeting your customers every day.

Make a list of the traits and skills you need, and then distill that down to a job description that you'll be able to use when you place the ad for the position.

Write Good Job Ads

Writing a good job ad is harder than it looks. Consider the differences between these examples:

Traditional

Administrative Assistant Wanted
Responsibilities include answering phones, scheduling appointments, typing medical reports,
data entry and filing. Experience in a busy medical office is a plus. $14 hourly. Send resume to xxxxxxxxx.

Alternative #1

Administrative Assistant Wanted
Are you great with people?
We are seeking a top-notch Administrative Associate. Are you professional, warm, tactful and just all around great with people? Are you organized and able to concentrate on details that are important to customers and staff? If so, and you're ready to join our growing business, email your resume and salary requirements to xxxxxxx. We'd love to hear from you!

Alternative #2:

Administrative Assistant Wanted
Do you have a voice that smiles and projects confidence? Can you handle multiple duties and prioritize in a fast-paced environment? Are you detail-oriented? Do you have impeccable spelling abilities, and can you write and speak clearly and concisely? Are you comfortable dealing with

strangers from all walks of life? Are you comfortable using the computer and learning new programs? Are you a self-starter? If so, send us your resume to xxxxxxxxx.

The traditional approach outlines responsibilities but says very little about the company, the culture and environment in which the person will be working in. The two alternatives both provide additional information simply in the way the job ads were written.

In your own job ads, show what your work environment is like and identify the personal traits you want from a candidate. The truth is if you convey a work environment that is attractive, you'll get a good selection of candidates who will want to work for you.

Review Resumes

Good resume writing is a challenging skill to learn, but as the business owner, your job is equally as difficult. Not only do you have to collect resumes from a variety of individuals, you also have to learn to sift through them to separate the wheat from the chaff.

Once the deadline for resume submission has passed, you'll have to review all of the cover letters and resumes to decide which ones are worth following up on with a preliminary phone interview.

There are a few key giveaways that show a job candidate is not right for your business. If the job requires them to communicate and/or read and write properly, any errors are a good sign that the candidate is not ideal, if only because they don't have the wherewithal to proofread their resume before sending it off. So errors are a dead giveaway as to sloppiness.

Incomplete or inaccurate information on the resume is unacceptable and should not be given any more consideration. It's unfortunate, but a lot of resumes are sent to potential employers without phone numbers and contact information. How are you supposed to contact that person? It also shows the candidate is not detail-oriented (a common criteria in many job descriptions).

If you're asking for specific information, technical requirements, a spoken or written language, or a set of skills, and they're not listed on the resume, then the candidate clearly doesn't fit the requirements you have set down. Don't try to force-fit a candidate that doesn't have the right skills because you think you could settle for them. If you ask for specific qualifications and they're not there, this is not the right person for you.

When it comes to hiring, business owners are often in panic mode, leading us to overlook resume red flags, but during the hiring process is the worst time to overlook such things. Don't grant a job interview to someone just because you're desperate; collect resumes to find the right candidate, not the "right now" one.

Preparing For The Interview

A job interview is a chance for you to meet and get a sense of the character of an employment candidate, but it's also a chance for that candidate to get a sense of you, your business and whether it's a place they would like to work. Don't miss the opportunity of recruiting top talent by treating the job interview casually or by not preparing for it.

Just as the interviewee should prepare for the formal job interview, the business owner (or whoever is responsible for hiring) should also prepare for the interview. Too many business owners don't give the job interview a second thought, and when it comes time for the interview, they're frazzled, hurried and flying by the seat of their pants. And it shows to the candidate.

To begin with, remind yourself about the interview ahead of time. Put it in your calendar. Well ahead of time, select a place in your office to conduct the interview. We always conducted interviews in the boardroom.

Set a maximum time for the interview. If you dedicate 40 minutes for each interview, don't go over that time, and plan ahead so you have the chance to ask all of the questions you want to and leave room for the candidate to ask you questions about the business and the work environment.

Preparing a list of questions will make the interview process go smoother. Although it's not what everyone uses, we used a mix of "classic" interview questions and analysis questions that gave an indication of how a person thought and reacted under pressure. We didn't want unthinking drones; we needed people who could think on their feet when things got busy. Analysis questions helped me weed out those who would not thrive in such a work environment.

In the end, remember that the purpose of the job interview is to measure people so you can find the best candidate for the role, rather than simply a warm body filling a seat.

The Phone Interview

Too many business owners treat the preliminary phone interview as simply a way to set up the in-person interview, but that's a wasted opportunity. While you have the candidate on the phone, it's an opportunity to get deeper into the candidate's personality.

Using the example of hiring for a receptionist, the phone interview is an excellent opportunity to undertake a pre-screening of the candidate. Do they have a pleasant phone manner? Are they articulate and appear to be engaged in the phone conversation? Do they come across professionally? It has been my experience that many people have a different personality on the phone than they do in person. If all goes well and no red flags go up, then go ahead and schedule an in-person job interview.

The Group Interview

Although we couldn't always do it, whenever possible we held group interviews at The Marketing Resource Group. A word of caution: Prior to initiating the group interview process, please check on privacy laws in your jurisdiction. The process for this is fairly simple. When the candidates arrived for their interview, they were ushered into the boardroom where other candidates were waiting. The reason we did this is to ensure that every candidate got all the same information delivered with the same enthusiasm from the company spokesperson.

When the time came to begin, I tried to put everyone at ease by being completely honest with them and explained the rationale for the group interview. In a nutshell, if you've ever gone through a day or two of interviewing people, you're aware of how quickly you can lose your enthusiasm for the process. Trying to stay upbeat and dynamic while repeating the same information over and over to each candidate is very difficult.

What the group interview provided to all the candidates was the opportunity to receive exactly the same information and delivered with the same enthusiasm. I also advised them that if what they heard about the company and the position was not to their liking that I appreciated their attendance.

After I had explained this to everyone, I then usually turned the process over to someone else in the company.

The One-on-One Interview

After the group interview, we would schedule one-on-one interviews, and for those, we took care to follow a process we had previously set up. We followed the process to the letter, and it's highly recommended you develop an interviewing process to keep a level of consistency and uniformity. It also makes it easier for the interviewers because they'll have gone through it several times.

Many people mistake the one-on-one interview as only being a discussion to see if the job candidate meets the requirements and is the ideal person to hire, but it's also the other way around -- a chance for the interviewee to measure the potential employer and decide if the job and company are the right fit for them. Just as you'd expect a job candidate to show up on time and dress appropriately, it's also important that interviewers follow a structure and process to give the candidate as much knowledge about your company and the way you do things to ensure a good fit.

However, a common and successful method to interviewing is often not followed. For the best results, have two people in the room with the job candidate. One keeps busy conducting the interview, while the other simply observes and takes notes. Since the active interviewer is so busy asking questions and discussing the job with the candidate, it's easier than you think to miss certain visual cues or misinterpret answers given by the candidate that should throw up red flags. Because the observer is doing only that, observing, they can pick up on these issues and make note of them.

After the interview is over, the two interviewers compare notes and make a decision as to continue pursuing the individual or let them go.

Hire Right

Everyone wants to find the best candidate, but too often small business owners are in a hurry or hire out of desperation. Do yourself a favor. Don't. Hiring is a time-consuming and costly process, and making a mistake is even more costly -- and it puts you back to square one, facing the entire process all over again.

Still, it's cheaper to do the process all over again than to hire wrong, so if the ideal candidate doesn't come along right away, don't panic. Continue looking.

Here are a few tips so that you hire the right people the first time:

- Take your time.
- Don't hire out of desperation.
- Project the image you want, so dress accordingly and choose a location for job interviews that reflects that image.
- Let job candidates do 80% of the talking during job interviews. Don't talk too much about how great your company is and remember they're selling you on why they should be selected and not the other way around. So ask the question, then be quiet and let the candidate talk. Otherwise, you may miss out on key facts and details about your candidates.
- Spend some time to learn about hiring and write processes around how your company hires people.

Interview Questions

There are ample resources available to source interview questions. Again, as part of your planning, you need to take time to research the types of questions you want to ask. You will want the questions to cover a range of topics relating to the company, the position and the individual. This is an opportunity to get a little creative with the questions. But this only happens if you take the time to formulate proper questions. Remember, if you plan on hiring more people in the future, taking the time to create good questions now will significantly reduce your preparation time in the future as many of the questions will become your standard for most of your interviews.

So here are just a few examples of questions I would ask:

1. What do you know about our company?

This question lets me know quickly whether the individual did any research on the company, as most of the information was available on our website.

2. What attracted you to this position?

This should give some insight into how much they thought about the position.

3. What section of the newspaper or what type of news do you prefer reading?

For me, the number one answer would be the business section or business news. Why? Because I want to hire people who are interested in business, and because this interest may bring ideas they read about to help my company.

4. If employed, why do you want to leave your current employer?

If the candidate starts whining and complaining about their current employer, it may be a cause for concern and indicate that this individual will never be satisfied.

5. Given the opportunity, what skill would you like to develop, and why? Personal or professional?

To me, this provides some insight into the individual's interests and motivations. The answer they give is not that important, but if they stumble to come up with a response, it would indicate to me that they really haven't given personal development much thought. I personally would prefer to hire individuals that are naturally predisposed to learning.

Thinking & Analyzing Questions

We also wanted to find people who could think on their feet and work under pressure. For that, we tossed a few thinking and analyzing questions into job interviews. Here are a few good ones:

1. Rearrange the following letters to make a word: N A C F E R
    Is the word the name of a city, state, country, animal or planet?

2. Which of the following letters is least like the other four?
    A F N Z E _____

3. Tom, at 12 years old, is three times as old as his brother. How old will Tom be when he is twice as old as his brother? 15 16 18 20 24

4. The price of an article was cut 20% for a sale. By what percentage must the article be increased to again to sell at the original price? 15% 20% 25% 30% 35%

5. Carol had some candy. After eating one piece, she gave half the remainder to her sister. After eating another piece, she gave half to her brother. If she has five candies left, how many did she start with? 11 22 23 25 32 _____

6. What is the average of the following: 6 + 12 + 10 + 4 + 3 = 35 5 7 8 3 _____

7. Bob must carry nine bricks from his truck to the backyard. He can only carry two bricks at a time. How many trips will he have to make? 4, 4.5, 5, 6 _____

8. A fish has a head nine inches long. The tail is equal to the size of the head plus one half the body. The body is equal to the size of the head and the tail. How many inches in total is the fish? 27 55 64 72

9. "Viscosity" has to do with: speed, distance, sound, thickness or color?

10. In a survey of 100 people, 61 responded yes, 17 responded no. What percentage is undecided? 10 12 20 22 25

11. Mary was 21 when her daughter Carol was born. Carol was 18 when her child was born. The child is now 6 years old. How old is Mary? 27 39 41 45 48 _____

12. How many orbits around the sun does the Earth make in 24 hours? None 1 2 3 4

13. If you are taking an IQ test, what does the IQ stand for?
    _____

    Individual quotation, Intelligence quotation, Intelligence quotient

14. There is a train that is one mile long, and it is traveling at a rate of one mile per hour through a tunnel that is one mile long. How much time will it take for the train to completely pass through the tunnel?

15. Why are manhole covers round?

Answers

Question		Question	
1	Country (France)	9	thickness
2	E	10	22
3	16	11	45
4	25%	12	none
5	23	13	intelligence quotient
6	7	14	2 hrs
7	5	15	so they won't fall in the hole
8	72		

8
Exit Strategy

"Define your own success. Figure out what's really important to you!"

- Greg Weatherdon

Build It To Sell It!

Here's what I tell small business owners: If you can't sell your business, you've only got a job.

So what do I mean by "you've only got a job?" It's quite simple, really. A job is performing work for someone else who, as your employer, usually dictates the who, what, when, where and why you are doing what you do. Rarely as an employee do you have the freedom to pick and choose what you want to do during a given day. In addition to not having the day-to-day freedom, you're typically only allocated a limited number of vacation days. I could go on, but you get the point. Unfortunately, many business owners

I encounter have an even more restrictive lifestyle than many employees. Is this why you went into business? I think not!

On the other hand, a saleable business affords the owner freedom of choice -- freedom to do pretty much what you want, when you want. We're not talking about a jet-setting lifestyle. No, it's the freedom to stay home for a day or just wake up and decide you'd rather spend the day on the golf course, and be able to do so knowing all is well back at the office.

Whether or not you ever sell your business doesn't matter, but when a business is built from day one so it can be sold, it makes it a lot easier for the owner to sell it if and when the time comes. A business that was built to serve the needs of the owner, rather than the other way around, is far more attractive to potential buyers. Building a business to sell places the business in a position to be sold relatively quickly should the opportunity arise, but more importantly, it allows the owner to live the life that most of us envision when we begin working for ourselves.

However, the typical small business owner has a tendency to get so wrapped up in the daily operations of the business that they are the cornerstone that holds the entire business together. Pull out that cornerstone, and the business collapses. Would you buy a business like that? Or would you pass it up and look for something that runs itself?

Making a business more attractive to potential buyers also goes hand-in-hand in getting more life out of your business and having the lifestyle you really want. As I've written previously, you should not be the hardest working person in your business.

As the owner of a business that has passed its start-up phase, it is time for you to think more strategically and less tactically, and the only way to do that is to start trusting your employees to do the work of actually managing the day-to-day operations of your enterprise.

Start Up Phase: Years 1 - 5

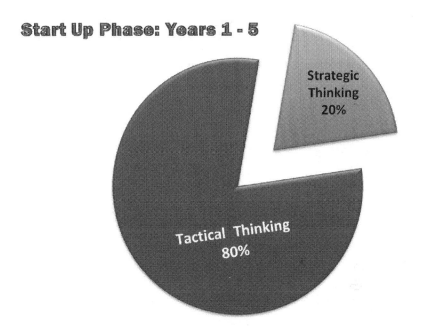

Strategic Thinking 20%

Tactical Thinking 80%

Post Start-Up : Years 5+

Strategic Thinking 80%

Tactical Thinking 20%

By getting your staff to handle as many of the day-to-day tasks for you -- and there are far more of these than you think -- you are now free to spend the necessary time to think about what you want to do with your business.

In order to truly achieve independence, you need to find the time to think strategically about your business. In other words, you need to work **on** your business and spend less time **in** your business.

Spending your time fostering relationships with key customers and suppliers or planning your exit strategy is a far more productive use of your time. Why? Chances are you will eventually grow restless, bored or -- and it happens frequently -- you'll reach burn-out. By putting the wheels in motion now, you'll position yourself and your company for when that day comes and you decide it's time to sell.

Let me ask you: Would you rather be working for your company or have your company working for you? I think we all know the answer.

Of course, the real question is: How do you get from being the hardest working employee in the business to the overall manager who makes the business work for your lifestyle? It's just like the question on how do you eat an elephant? One bite at a time!

The same applies to getting out from under your business. You do it one step at a time.

Planning Your Exit

What's your exit strategy? Do you even have one? To many business owners, planning their exit strategy is like writing a will. It's something they know they should do, but figure they can do it later.

Unfortunately, some day you're going to decide it's time to sell your company and only then will you realize that the company is not in any condition to sell, let alone command the price you want. Conversely, you may be one of those owners who say they never plan to retire. But that doesn't absolve you from creating an exit strategy. You may wonder why you need an exit strategy if you're never planning to retire. In a word, illness! An unforeseen illness could easily derail your plans and, if such an event were to happen, how would you be able to convert your business assets into financial assets that you or your family may need to live on?

There are plenty of other resources to consult regarding proper insurance coverage or family succession planning, and I have no intention of delving into those areas. In addition, who you sell to or how you go about the selling process also won't be covered. My job here is simply to get you thinking about the process and the things you need to put in place if you are ever in a position to sell your business.

What I want you to consider is the practical necessity of building and organizing your business as though you are going to sell it. I know you understand the benefits of such a strategy, but for many of you, you just can't justify focusing on it because you have too many other more pressing priorities. This is where you're wrong. Building your business with the goal of selling it can actually free up a tremendous amount of your time. In turn, you can use this free time to do as you wish and get more life out of your business.

Regardless of what you think today, many of you are going to wake up one morning and realize you want out and it's time to sell. The decision to sell usually happens very suddenly and you'll find yourself somewhat impatient and wanting it to get it done very quickly. It's happened to me and thousands of other business owners, so I urge you to prepare now.

Chances are many of you spend some of your time daydreaming about selling your business and being free. But usually that's where it ends because reality sets in and you have to get back to running your business. On top of that, the distraction of running your business also

helps you to avoid thinking about how you would actually go about selling your business.

Selling a business is not like anything else you've done and is a slow, time-consuming process. Unlike selling your house, you can't bring in a house stager to make everything beautiful in a couple of days.

The harsh reality is if your business is not in a saleable state, it can take you the better part of two years to get it ready to be put up for sale. If that isn't bad enough, it can easily take another two years to sell your business. That's when you begin to see the light. The deal requires you to stay on for another two years in a transitional period. So when you add it all up, an unprepared business may require your involvement for an additional six years from the time you decide to sell until you're finally free.

If things aren't bad enough, it is estimated that upwards of three-quarters of the businesses that are listed for sale will not get sold. Building your business to sell from the start is far easier than trying to reorganize it when you really only want to get out.

How Do You Know It's Time To Sell?

Most small business owners wake up one day and decide they've had enough, but it's rarely an overnight decision. What has happened is they've missed or dismissed the cues along the way. If you keep an eye out for certain behaviors or changes, then you may see your exit coming:

- Boredom is the most frequent cause for business owners wanting out. For whatever reason, the passion they once felt for running their business has vanished and been replaced by a general malaise they can't seem to shake.

- The business doesn't challenge them any more. Eventually all the fun and challenge may be gone. Entrepreneurs tend to like a challenge, so when a venture is no longer offering that, it may be time to move on.

- Rules and regulations change. Even age-old business sectors run the risk of having new rules and regulations thrust upon them that forces them to adapt. Sometimes business owners can handle it, and sometimes they feel nothing but frustrated. Their role becomes a chore instead of a joy.

Look for these cues of boredom, frustration and lack of challenge. If you're starting to feel them, you may be heading towards the end of your time as owner of your business. If you can't do anything to change your attitude, it's probably time to start thinking about selling.

Why Doesn't The Business Sell?

As I mentioned earlier in this chapter, three-quarters of businesses listed for sale will not be sold. The odds of selling aren't very good, but knowing why your business isn't selling will go a long way towards making sure you're one of the minority that is successful.

Here are the most common reasons why a business does not sell:

- The selling price is too high. Most owners don't get their businesses appraised when they decide to sell. They slap a price tag on their enterprise that is frequently far too high and nothing more than wishful thinking and not grounded on market realities. A business appraisal is not cheap, but getting one done will tell you what dollar figure you should be asking for. It's a huge negotiating advantage because you will be dealing from a position of strength that supports your asking price.

- The business can't run without you. The entire reason for this book is to help you make your business work for you rather than the other way around. If you micro-manage or otherwise manage your business in a way that means the company is totally dependent on you, then why would anybody buy it?

- The business may simply not be viable. Perhaps it was at some point, but every industry has its ups and downs, and maybe the outlook on your industry is not attractive. The new owner will want to see solid evidence that they can grow the business. Sunset industries are not very appealing.

Would You Buy Your Company?

The dream for many entrepreneurs is to sell their businesses and then retire. But when I ask these same people if knowing what they know about their company, would they buy it, I get very few that answer in the affirmative. So why is that?

For the most part, it appears that the majority had not really spent a lot of time thinking about selling their companies. They've been too busy with all the other duties and responsibilities necessary to build the business that they just assumed someone, some day would buy.

From day one, selling your business should be one of your top objectives. This way, everything you do in organizing your business and its processes will be geared towards ultimately selling your business. As I mentioned earlier, don't wait until you're burnt out and need to sell immediately.

How do you do it? First off, put yourself in the buyer's position. What would you want a company that you were thinking of buying to look like? Some of my criteria would be the following:

- Recurring and predictable revenue from existing accounts (as much as that's possible).
- Customer longevity.
- Low staff turnover.
- Dependable and responsible employees.
- A delegated business, where the onus is not always on the owner.
- Owner's freedom -- to be able to concentrate on those things you enjoy doing.

So if your current business doesn't measure up to the things you'd be looking for if you were buying your business, you need to start making changes. Because if you can't sell your business, you've only got a job.

Made in the USA
Columbia, SC
18 August 2019